THE ENTREPRENEUR THAT COULD:
What American Entrepreneurs Need To Know For the New Economy

by Casey Jurado
copyright 2010

www.TheEntrepreneurThatCould.com

Dedicated to all the entrepreneurs that made this country great and to those who can make it great again.

****

We can have either democracy in this country or we can have great wealth concentrated in the hands of a few, but we cannot have both . -Louis Brandeis, Supreme Court Justice

****

I am a most unhappy man. I have unwittingly ruined my country. A great industrial nation is now controlled by a system of credit. We are no longer a government by free opinion, no longer a government by conviction and a vote of the majority, but a government by the opinion and duress of a small group of dominant men." President Woodrow Wilson six years after signing into law the Federal Reserve Act.

The Entrepreneur That Could   *Casey Jurado*

Reader's comments:

Loved the book as well as the references to the integrity and idea of what America was to the founding fathers. It gave me a reflection of then and now. What would the founding fathers think of the corrupt corporate influences that now challenge Democracy and their brilliant idea called "America". The book encouraged me to ask myself "What can I do about it?" A thought provoking read!
Joyce Calhoun

You probably don't know Casey, and so you have not had an opportunity to talk to him. That's a pity, because Casey is a thinking man. In a world with so few people who take the time to think, someone who does easily stands out. Read this book because by doing so you will become a thinking person.

You're not an entrepreneur? That's OK. The entrepreneur word has deeply touched your life; Casey lays this out for you so you can see it and make decisions about it. You may not agree with what he has written, and that's OK. Of course he wants agreement, but more important to Casey is that after you have read and thought your way to the end of the book that you at least understand why you believe what you do. Fasten your seat belt and enjoy the ride.
Teddy L. Nation

Casey Jurado's observations and perspectives open your mind so that you will not be able to close it in quite the same way again. The point of view comes from a distillation of information gathered from the outer reaches away from the center. It allows for the development of a view from another window, on an upper floor, from where the same things we've seen everyday, and known, look surprisingly and disturbingly different. It seems that we have gotten a peek behind the curtains and it is impossible to forget what we've seen. Disneyland has caught fire and burnt to the ground and what are we to do?!
Michael Krapes Psy.D.

The ETC contains lots of interesting observations on our modern society, the interaction in society and the contribution/destruction caused by different businesses. I really liked the concept of Business Common Sense. How true that you can be a MBA or engineering genius and still not be able to start or run a profitable business. In many cases, BCS is more important than capital or a formal education in determining success. Casey seems a little harsh on large corporations without which we would not have most of the great developments in science, medicine, and products available today. But I do agree that many neglect their obligations to protect scarce resources throughout the world. Great book, Casey!
John Merritt

After reading Casey's well thought-out book and having some time to contemplate the issues mentioned, I think the primary problem comes back to greed. Not only on the part of the RCMC's, but on the part of the consumers who have become ever-expectant of the lowest prices possible. In expecting cheap food and products we have ultimately defined the methods in which the RCMC's produce what we consume.

If we want to have healthy foods, we must accept the higher prices to produce them. If we wish to provide a basic level of human existence, we must inform ourselves as to where and how our consumer items are produced. We can demand the standards outlined in this book by supporting those systems which provide them by using our consumer power. Once that is achieved, we will see our demands become standard policy and prices will adjust to accommodate the demand. It requires ongoing effort on our part to become and remain aware of how our foods and goods are produced and to act according to our own ethics and expectations.
Susan LeVeque

Table of Contents

2010, CSE (Common Sense Era)

Entrepreneurism in America is sick. Indeed, all of our institutions are at grave risk. Entrepreneurs and employees are overworked, multi-stimulated and out of balance, struggling to make the system work.

The reason is simple: business techniques revolve around the methods, capital and environment created by the most powerful corporations NOT common sense or genuine community needs.

Multinational corporations dictate and refine our leisure options and our conforming appearances. Forces of division create endless distinctions, separating us from members of our community. Headlines daily declare new realities and our experts prognosticate dire consequences. As our world shifts under our feet, it's no wonder that we doubt our own self-definition. Grasping for something we can believe in, we identify with where we live, what we drive, which brands we buy and shout sports team pride. But what do these have to do with what makes life meaningful and lasting in America?

The Entrepreneur That Could (ETC) is about regaining our course. It is a business/ life philosophy based on common sense. Common sense is simple, but as life's complexities exploded in an urban industrial society, we got separated from communal food production and the cycles of Nature. That's how "common sense" got less common.

I believe common sense can revolutionize our business paradigm. What is missing in most business approaches these days is a lack of insight that comes from common sense. Common sense is telling me (and many other American business owners) that the current business paradigm isn't working and is taking us down. It won't take just a few tweaks to fix it. Luckily, we have inspiration for this awakening from the Founding Fathers and the Declaration of Independence.

ETC will step back around 200 years, to the early days that formed this nation's principles. Although our country's founders were imperfect, they lived by common sense and common sense proved their point. They observed that the monarchies and aristocracies were corrupt. They understood that monopolies like the East India Trading Company that supplied their teas and spices were impositions on free trade. They studied nature's cycles and ways, and experimented to invent new ways of improving the general welfare. They observed how power corrupts and discussed at great lengths how to stop that particular insanity in this land of new opportunity.

As we revisit the Founding Fathers, we discover that they were more than authors of the Declaration of Independence, the Bill of Rights or the US Constitution. They were business people, farmers, self-educated intellectuals, tradespeople, scientists, diplomats and entrepreneurs.

ETC will help readers, as they start to recreate their reality for our new age of opportunity, to think more like the Founding Fathers. This new reality will not be like the old one any more than the Founding Fathers wanted a "New Britain." Nor will it be what the world's dominating corporations want. This new reality must be right for us as free individuals, our local economies and communities...

America and the planet, by extension.

Americans that I talk to are ready to throw off the controls of self-interested corporations, intolerant institutional religions and compromised governments. We want to take responsibility for our future instead of going where the world corporations and their puppet governments are taking us. It is time to forge into the future using tools of character and entrepreneurism that we call "ETC, The Entrepreneur That Could."

ETC is

- defining who we are
- deciding where we are going
- using common sense
- getting smart about money
- being disciplined physically and mentally
- commiting to personal and community integrity
- being connected to Nature and her cycles
- taking responsibility for our behavior
- always hopeful and inventive and
- stopping the insanity (or at least, enjoying it more).

I have no intentions of taking sides or making enemies on the road to a better, more community-connected future. Yes, some will take issue with ETC. That's okay. But let's agree to promise two things: to choose to tell the truth over being politically correct AND to state our positions as clearly as possible. From this exchange, it is my hope that you, the reader, are able to see what is happening so you can decide where you want to go.

If you know of Louis CK, you might have heard his comedic sketch about being stuck in traffic. The backup was solid steel for miles. No one was going anywhere anytime soon. You know the situation yourself if you have lived in an urban or suburban setting. Then out of the blue, the driver behind Louis started honking his horn. Louis wondered what this could mean. Couldn't the man in back see that Louis couldn't move if his life depended on it? OK, so he is frustrated, so am I, thought Louis. But the honking continued. As the noise became more than irritating Louis heard the man demanding that Louis "Go!" Instead, he just sat there, blocked like everyone else.

In the midst of the aggravation, Louis got an idea. Instead of exchanging insults, he decided to have his argument, not the argument the man in back wanted to have. "Hey!" Louis exploded as he approached the car in back, "Where's my jacket?" "Huh?" "You heard me, you got my jacket! I want it now! Give it me!" The man got scared, quickly rolled up his windows and locked the doors. The honking stopped. Louis preferred his argument.

There are powerful corporations that now control the majority of television and newspapers, automobiles, real estate, food production and distribution, fashion, cosmetics, publishing, household appliances, telephone and every aspect of infrastructure. We have heard and seen their argument. Now it's time for ours. We want to know what they have done with our environment, our government, our freedom, our ability to earn a living, our economy, our children's education, our medical care, our food and water quality...and our future. That's the argument we are going to have. It's our future and our health at stake.

ETC will tell you what you are not reading in the press but might verify by observation. Why is this important? If you are going to take a different path than the one laid out for you, know what you are dealing with. Read that in Sections One and Two.

ETC offers entrepreneurs a foundational philosophy that I have learned from other successful entrepreneurs. Their successes did not come from hard work, but an easy, intuitive approach enhanced with common sense. In many cases, these successful individuals had no college. With or without a business degree, this will expand your awareness of the cycles of business and be successful in the age of niche markets. I want to thank each role model for inspiring me to share the principles of the Entrepreneur That Could. Study Sections Three, Four, Seven and Supplement One.

ETC celebrates who we are. We are inventive and community-based. And, if we are to survive, we must be integrated with Nature. Section Five will open your eyes regarding our all-important reliance on Nature.

The RCMCs (Resource Controlling Multinational Corporations) will appear throughout the book. They are largely responsible for our modern and post-modern lifestyles. Mostly, I will point out how the food industry has been re-engineered. Just keep in mind that the RCMCs have done this in countless other industries. Read Sections One, Two, Six and Seven.

The Entrepreneur That Could is about living on a planet with only a few continental land masses. These lands may seem expansive to an individual trekking it on foot. But not all of it gives us food, water and resources for life. This is all we have. There isn't another Earth in the galaxy supermarket. The way I see it, consumerism is not a winning strategy for this planet. Our future is in responsible, ethical and commonsensical entrepreneurism. The healthy, and balanced ETC choice is about to be unfolded before you.

Read <u>ETC</u>:

1. because it will help you understand the world and your place in it,
2. to discover principles of entrepreneurial success in the new economy,
3. because it is time for an age of common sense, and
4. because, in your heart, you know it's true.

These are the times that try men's souls. The summer soldier and the sunshine patriot will, in this crisis, shrink from the service of their country; but he that stands now, deserves the love and thanks of man and woman...but he whose heart is firm, and whose conscience approves his conduct, will pursue his principles unto death. – Thomas Paine, patriot, founding father.

Section One, Taking Stock: You are here.

America the Beautiful

"America the Beautiful" is something I used to take at face value. But like many people around the world, I have become disillusioned and pragmatic. No longer can I believe in the American Dream we inherited, that the government is on our side or that the Resource Controlling Multinational Corporations (the RCMCs) invest to bring us fulfillment via burger clowns, fast cars and easy retirement options. No. Life in America no longer makes common sense.

11

But seen another way, Americans are in an awkward stage of opportunity amidst accelerated change. To illustrate, here is a partial list of changes and opportunities from a mere 100 years ago. (My apologies for being long on detail.)

The year is 1910

More people live in rural areas than cities; suburbs are uncommon.

The average US wage in 1910 is 22 cents per hour. In 2010's economy, that would equal $4.85

The average U.S. worker earns less than $14 per week, working from 54 to 60 hours.

An unskilled laborer, who works twelve-hour days, seven days a week, cannot support a family of five. Children work and some are the household breadwinners.

The average US worker makes between $400 and $650.00 per year. In 2010's economy, that would equal $6,000 to 9,000 per year.

Sugar costs four cents a pound. 2010's money = 88 cents per pound

Coffee is fifteen cents a pound. 2010's money = $3.13 per pound.

70% of U. S. bread is baked at home.

Conditioners and shampoos do not exist on the market, so to clean their hair most people brush it.

Because hospitals are so feared, more than 95 percent of all births take place at home. Doctors make house calls.

Midwives deliver half of all babies born in the United States.

Abortions are common and inexpensive, ten dollars being the standard rates in New York and Boston.

The Five leading causes of death in 1910 are:
1. Heart disease

2. Pneumonia and influenza

3. Tuberculosis

4. Diarrhea

5. Stroke

Life expectancy in the United States has reached 48.4 years for men and 51.8 years for women.

Divorces are becoming more common and within five years, the US will have the highest divorce rate in the world, with one in seven marriages ending in divorce.

Telephony is in its infancy. Telephone calls are handled by operators (dialers do not exist yet) and cross country calls are impossible.

The entire United States has about 1,000 miles of paved roads.

The American flag has 46 stars.

The population of Las Vegas, Nevada is 945.

Crossword puzzles, canned beer, and iced tea haven't been invented yet. Sliced bread, bikinis, bras and ballpoint pens are unheard of.

There is no Mother's Day or Father's Day.

One out of fourteen adults can't read or write and most children quit school after 8th grade.

Marijuana, heroin, and morphine are all available over the counter at the local corner drugstores. Pharmacists recommend them believing that 'Heroin clears the complexion, gives buoyancy to the mind, regulates the stomach and bowels, and is, in fact, a perfect guardian of health.'

Commercial air traffic does not exist and pilots fly without (still uninvented) parachutes.

The change our great grandparents went through brought opportunities galore: jobs, knowledge, investments, science, entertainment, goods and services...and the same is true today.

We have come a long way, Baby...along with some substantial slippage from our roots.

Back home in 2010 USA

Today, Americans are often told (and we feel inclined to believe until recently), that America is the best place on Earth. We believed that our social programs were the best; our health care, safety, economy, and prospects are the best here. That may have been true a few years ago, but it is no more. American cities are no longer rated as the best places in the world to live. The World Quality of Life Index rates countries for culture, leisure, environment, safety and weather. France, Australia, Switzerland, Germany, New Zealand and Luxembourg were rated ahead of the US for 2010. The US fell from 3rd to 7th as a result of the economic chaos in 2009. Britain fell from 20th to 25th. Additional studies by other groups confirm this lapsed state.

Do we have it good in America? Yes. We're driving cars where we want to go. We are living in dry, warm houses, drinking fresh water. We're going to concerts, going to the beach or ballpark. We're jumping on planes and traveling around the world. When we get sick, we go to hospitals and we're benefiting from some of the best medical technology on the planet. We can buy from clothing to jewelry at Macy's or Wal-mart. Mobile phone choices go beyond AT&T and Verizon. We buy groceries at Whole Foods or

Albertson's. We shop at the mall or online.

Are we going to be able to perpetuate this lifestyle? With all those benefits and conveniences? With the current use of resources?[1]

The answer is No. We already know that. Our lifestyle is unsustainable.[2] So, certain change is coming. Change is always good when the community can adapt with care for one another, when we know who we are and where we want to go. And the good news is that this coming shift is loaded with opportunities for our future entrepreneurs.

The economic decline and its opportunities

It was recently reported by the Associated Press that one out of seven homes valued over a million dollars in the US is either in tax default or mortgage default. While we can't get inside their heads, it is reasonable to assume that the owners of these homes are not willing to put their cash into them, even though they have money in the banks. At least 14% (one in seven) of the monied middle class knows that

---

[1]   The artwork of rampant consumerism by artist Chris Jordan is also enlightening. ChrisJordan.com, .TED.com and on YouTube.
[2]   For a quirky view of our consumerist lifestyle, visit The Story of Stuff. www.StoryofStuff.com

it doesn't make intelligent financial sense to throw money after a devalued piece of real estate- even if it is their home.

One of the next big fall-outs will involve commercial shopping centers. The economy is coming to grips with a situation where it cannot support the lifestyle it used to offer. These structures were built on assumptions of cheap transportation, plenty of disposable income and free time to shop. Opportunities will be available here as well.

We didn't see it coming.

In truth, we didn't see this coming. Even the upper classes didn't. We've been blinded by convenience, regularity, low cost, and abundance. It's not just the housing market that got valued for more than it is worth. The economy, Wall Street, banks, big box stores and malls, auto manufacturers and more are also overvalued. If there ever was a time to begin taking personal responsibility for our food, clothing and shelter, it is NOW. Taking responsibility is the new opportunity.

You know, on one hand you have to hand it to the RCMCs. They did their homework. They have extensively studied the earth, markets, delivery systems, engineering, chemistry, agriculture, biology, psychology, propaganda, motivation, manipulation and the influence of mass media. They discovered how to skew facts to influence their customers and clients, how to create addicted customers, how to use the system to be legally fair and still make Wall Street stealing respectable. They studied efficiency and how to manufacture reality. Now we are dependent on their standards and rules of business.

Most particularly for the illustrative purposes here, the RCMCs have taken a leading role in changing the way we eat. According to the documentary "Food, Inc.," "In the last 50 years, our food has changed more than it has for the last ten thousand years." And while fifty years ago we could buy a few mass-produced packaged foods like Coca-Cola, Heinz catsup, and Jay's potato chips, our current choices at the market are predominantly products full of chemical additives that mimic flavor, manage texture and "tooth," and create hunger and addiction. Besides mass-produced industrial foods available at most restaurants, we also have several choices of fast food franchises almost anywhere we live.

The agriculture departments in many universities such as Iowa State and Michigan State have been funded to develop ways to boost production from two to ten times the amount of corn and soybeans farmers could produce 50 years ago. All over America, millions of tons of food are efficiently processed in bulk, packaged and delivered to distribution centers called supermarkets and restaurants. When you realize that this system feeds most of the 311 million residents in the US, day after day, in and out of season, this efficiency is mind-boggling.

This efficiency of space and labor, combined with trade incentives, allows us to have our coffee every morning, a quick and easy breakfast of boxed cereal with pasteurized milk (or drive-through sandwich) and drive on roads built for delivery trucks in our fashionable car. You've got to hand it to the creators of this. It looks like it works, even when it doesn't account for the social, ecological, personal and family costs of being disassociated from our food source.

As good as it looks, we know something is wrong.

Combine misinformation on the public airwaves with general public confusion, the demands of everyday business to pay the bills and finish endless household chores, people readily unwind in front of the TV. They believe that they worked hard and deserve to be relaxed and "comfortably numb" on the couch.[3] Weekends are often spent following community sports for the kids or professional sports on TV, between loads of laundry, catnaps, reading magazines, house cleaning and upkeep.

Look at our educational system to see what is wrong.

Don't get me wrong, some of my best friends are teachers. They are great people. But they must teach what they are told to teach. And the problem isn't what they *are* teaching. It is what they *aren't* teaching.

What they aren't teaching results in a less educated nation and students less equipped for marketplace realities. We are now 13th in the world in reading and worse in most subjects like math, science, geography and history. Our children are not being taught about family, personal responsibility, entrepreneurial initiative, common sense or logic, geography, our political system, self reliance, nature, nutrition, diplomacy, personal finance or great literature that inspires independent thinking and action. That is a large deficit.

In the early 1900's, public debate centered on what the

---

[3] Pink Floyd's "Comfortably Numb" refers to Roger Water's being "comfortably numb" on heroin. It is an apt metaphor for our consumerist culture, in my humble opinion.

curriculum should be for the new public high schools. Eventually, it was the industrial sector that won the debate. More than anything, they needed young people to be trained for mass production. The new schools used mass production techniques to create graduates that would meet the needs of industry and schools haven't changed much since.

I see our present school system as a program to create graduates of "Ten Years Dumb." "Ten Years Dumb" means that as soon as you graduate from high school, the credit card industry is ready to sign you up, the auto industry has your number and every other whim can be satisfied because the consumerist culture is already embedded in you. If you graduate at 18, then at 28 you are likely still bumbling around, and now you have at least ten more years of getting out of the debt you took on because you weren't educated in school about personal finance. Obscene profits for the RCMCs are *guaranteed* this way.

Kids are not taught to ask questions, to challenge the status quo or to be creative. Art and music may be the only things taught in school that allow for individual expression. And funding for those activities is slipping away. Do you know what else they are teaching in school? If you are hungry, go get a Hostess cupcake in the courtyard. If you are having a slump or you have a learning disorder, try a Coke for a lift. Schools should be about gaining knowledge and wisdom, not catering to solutions created for us by the owners of the company store.

Sports teams for kids are another nightmare. I know this will be unpopular for those that believe that sports participation teaches teamwork. I have seen another view. Kid's sports teams teach our kids to be losers. School and community sports teams make it very clear: failure is bad and it is unacceptable. This, however, does not necessarily translate as an incentive to win, though it has potential to teach some to win at all costs. A game should be a collective celebration of skill and development. Yet what we hear from the coaches and team members is "You did it wrong, J.J." "Sandy, you should have caught that ball!" "What were you thinking, Bobby?" "Terry, we might have won the game if it wasn't for you!" With this lesson in mind, children become more afraid of failure, less likely to take risk as an individual thinker, or later, as an entrepreneur. Sports training as we do it promotes two things: slipping into the mainstream and playing according to the rules that set us up for failure.

A simple look at any public school classroom through a child's eyes will tell you what is important to the makers of the rules. Children sit in the classroom or school library and compare that to the movie theatre, the sports arenas, the entertainment centers, the amusement parks...even the Wal-marts- and they can see what matters to grownups. It isn't school buildings. It isn't books. And it isn't education.

News Flash. Political Sides Taken.

We find ourselves today struggling with others over complex and divisive national and world issues. Taxes. Immigration. Fat cats in government and corporations. Environmental disasters. Government bailouts. Real estate crashes. Unemployment. But are those the real issues? Let's just take the issue of immigration. It is a hot topic as I write this book and recently I was asked what I thought regarding the burden of illegal immigrants on schools, hospitals and other civic resources.

Here was my answer: "Yes, illegal aliens make demands on public schools and hospitals. And yes, some are paying income taxes, or at least buying groceries, gas, electronics, mobile phones...all of which are taxed. They are adding revenue to the economy, if not exactly the way registered aliens do. But, for sake of argument, let's take the illegals out of the equation. Let's say that none are in the country...they have all left. Now, let's look at what we have. Are our tax, health care or education problems solved? Are fewer small businesses failing? Is our state now out of debt? Is the war over? No. We still have the same masters, the large international corporations. They benefit when we think that our illegals, or some oil spill, or our failing economy are the issues because when issues are made political, people will square off and fight one another over how to solve it. And no one really sees the man behind the curtain.

I think our problems are way beyond immigration. What really threatens the American Dream includes:

- political factions that argue over turf instead of rational analysis,
- the American political process that buckles to Corporate interests,
- our lack of unity and community,
- our disconnection with the Earth,
- the confusion brought to us by the Corporate-run media,
- our disabled educational systems,

- our willingness to be bribed by convenience, new fashions and gizmos and not least of these,
- our lack of common sense.

Even the self-help industry is complicit in our modern and unsustainable paradigm. It keeps trying to tell us how to fit and succeed in a society that has very little basis in reality. Self-help gurus take advantage of our flawed economic and established business models. They tell us to stand on our own two feet, knowing that there is precious little support in our communities. Self-help books and recordings are ignorant as to why families are breaking up at unprecedented rates or why homelessness is epidemic. They do not examine the causes of failed business ventures or joblessness. They challenge their audiences to forge ahead in spite of collapsing environments and bailout after bailout of the country's largest employers, banks and failed governmental fix-ups.

Independent news

The greatest gift Nature blessed us with is the ability to think independently and rationally. The Founding Fathers understood this and struggled to create an environment free of unnecessary constraints on independent pursuits. The soil they tilled was a healthy mix for growing a self-reliant people, free of unnatural additives like monopolistic corporations, manipulative central governments and influential institutionalized religions.

When we don't use this gift of independent thought, we become prey for legitimate appearing organizations that promise financial rewards, leisure time, a vote in government, goods for cheap or spiritual retirement. We fall for promises of free money without doing any work (high interest), paid vacations, free medical care and quiet final days in retirement.

And without our connection to reality, especially with Nature's possibilities and limits, we cannot be independent or think independently. Without Nature, we are living in a fictitious reality. Without living in the real world created by nutritious food, clear air, clean water and the sunshine we require, common sense becomes our forgotten asset.

He said, she said.

The powers that be are going to find fault with and discount this material. But this is not because the material is flawed. Their disagreement will not be about the need for having common sense, nor about having a different business perspective. Whatever issue they raise, read between the lines. Their purpose is and always will be, to use others' platforms to restate their own agenda. But, sorry "guys," this is our argument. All ETC proposes is a newly designed, community involved, common sense ethic, based on observable facts.

This is not time to listen to their layers of "shinola." (You know, the layers are multiple.) We know what it is, we can observe it and we need to speak the truth. Let us not be detained by debates over, say, whether global warming is a public concern, the public posting of the biblical commandments or who will win the World Series. Because if we just tread water or if we don't resist the monopolistic forces, everything the RCMCs have put in place will continue their course. (See Section Two.) More wars to capture resources. More lies from the media, government and the Treasury. More bailouts of a sick economy. More national debt. Tighter control of citizenry. (We already have the largest prison population per capita in the world!) Rising inflation. Poorer quality and less food. Higher medical costs. More polluted streams, oceans, lakes and air...

Why I wrote this book and what you can expect.

More than anything, it is my goal to help concerned Americans, especially entrepreneurs, to understand the real situation we are in. Most Americans don't know. I get asked, "What is this and how did we get here?" They know something is wrong. Most are aware of the deceit but aren't sure what to believe. Our belief systems don't seem to be able to put together a logical framework for what is happening.

I wrote this book to clear up where we are. As our economy fails us, it will do us good to see what opportunities lie in the new American economy.

In Section Two, we will explore how where the RCMCs will take us if we do nothing, where the Founding Fathers would guide us and why niche markets are the new wave of opportunity.

Section One Summary: We have arrived at a new America that is failing us on many levels. Chief among the change agents are the Resource Controlling Multinational Corporations (RCMCs). They have changed the way we eat, educate, work, pay taxes and what we buy. Further challenging our American Dream is our disconnection from nature and community, our willingness to be bribed by convenience and be entertained by corporate-run media. ETC proposes a newly designed, community involved, common sense ethic based on a holistic approach. With that, we can move toward new opportunities for entrepreneurial growth.

Adversity makes men and prosperity makes monsters. – Victor Hugo, author, playwright

Section 2, Where Are We Going?

Entrepreneurial minds want to know.

You are invited.

You are cordially invited to one of the greatest shifts in the history of humankind. It is right here, right now. We have arrived at a place where the industrial and technological activities on the planet are clashing with the natural environmental cycles of the planet.

We have been told that this is the case, and many of us believe it, but societal trends and the life of the rich and famous expose the binge we are on and that we feel helpless to stop.

Is it okay with you that:

- We are disinclined to give up our cars, drive at lower speeds, carpool or limit our trips?

- We buy energy saving appliances but only because we enticed by reduced cost?
- We are slow to invest in alternative energy for our offices and homes?
- We continue to buy on credit when it comes at crippling rates?
- We participate in elections that we know are lopsided by corporate greed?
- We let the government step in to resolve our local problems as they trample on our rights?
- We will not commit to supporting local farms that offer us the most healthy meat and produce?
- We ignore common sense solutions like proactive health care, nutrition and living within our means?
- We depend on the media for entertainment and information and ignore our neighbor's company and wisdom?
- We allow ourselves to be dependent on soulless mega-corporations to fulfill our most basic needs?

But there's more:

- It's the buildup of toxic wastes and plastics.
- It's the economic bubble built on dreams of avarice rather than hard assets and human services.

- It's the loss of freedom in America and the growth of America's prison population.
- It's the mad grab to capture and control life forms that make up you and me.
- It's our loss of connection with Nature, the source of life.
- It's our withdrawal of financial support for anything that does not have a proven value in the marketplace.
- It's our willingness to be seduced by convenience, cheap goods, political ineptitude and public indebtedness.

What Would Wisdom Say?

I have spent many enjoyable hours learning from living models of success. Luckily, many of these people are friends, family and classmates. (You will find their inspiring stories in the Niche Market Supplement.) As much as I have learned from them, it would be hard to say that anyone has inspired me more than the Founding Fathers. It is their spirit of entrepreneurism that established this nation. What would *they* say if they were invited to this great shift? If they were to rise from their silence and speak to the country they founded?

Here is a summary of what I think the brightest and the best of them (Ben Franklin, John Adams, Thomas Jefferson, George Washington and Thomas Paine) would conclude. I think it is interesting that they put "the citizenry" before "the government."

The Citizenry:

- Too many Americans do not question authority and do not think for themselves. They do not apply their inventiveness to America's viability and greatness; their inventiveness is primarily for personal gain alone.
- Americans worship at churches that have compromised their credibility by their political and economic involvement.
- A citizen's ability and right to earn an income is not taxable.
- The public is generally weak and unwell from their comforts and poor diet.
- When Americans do not actively protect their right to address the government for grievances, their governments will take away

their freedom.

- Americans seem to have forgotten that they grant the government the right to rule; the government does not grant citizens the rights to participate.

Community Discourse:

- How is community discourse possible when Americans don't even know their neighbors on the same street or living in the same building?
- Political correctness has given way to impotence.
- Political discourse, when hosted by the government, is always far from being open and enlightened.

The Government:

- The government often operates without the consent of common people and has restricted the public's rights to make their government answerable to the majority.
- The right to bear arms against a cruel and oppressive government is little threat to a

government with air superiority, better ammunition, advanced communications and effective media manipulation. Allowing the government to spend money on propaganda, advanced weapons and surveillance also gives them permission to be more powerful than the citizenry.

- The poor in America do not receive the "justice" available to the rich. Each person's rights to a fair trial are conditioned these days by their financial resources and connections.

- The federal government now governs more by policy than law. Within that policy, non-citizens have advantages that are not available to American-born citizens.

The Natural Surroundings:

- Where did all the natural beauty go? Why is most of it cleared and paved over? How can you live like this?

- America's most powerful corporations pay people to upset, subdue and overcome Nature rather than work with and respect it.

- Clearly, access to buildings is more important to today's Americans than the country's natural resources.
- The production of toxic chemicals and substances fails the test of common sense. The poor pay the biggest toll. It must stop if only for moral reasons.
- Enjoyment of Nature seems largely limited to the use of Nature and not its restoration. What is taken must be returned; it is Nature's highest law.

The Economy:

- The economy is flawed because it is based on debt, not on common value.
- And why is it that those with more assets than they need use it to create class, privilege and empires? We would ask, 'Who gave them the opportunity to earn and collect these assets? The community! It is your give-back to invest it there, not in speculative betting.'
- Americans are so in debt to others and the future that the country's independence is

compromised. It is individual Americans that will be required to pay the debt, not some elected government body or credit based banking system.

- There is apparently no accounting for the limits of nonrenewable resources.
- The economic system is too highly regulated in a bias against the middle and poor classes.

Schooling:

- Schooling does not prepare the country's youthful resource for practical life tasks or self reliance. It keeps them impotent, dependent, uncritical and in debt.
- Public schooling is effective in spitting out consumers and followers of fads. In brief, youngsters are ignorant about the community, nature, the country and the world.
- Today's schools teach the young to study to earn a job placement that is dependent on an employer and not to develop their mind, understand the value of innovation, build character or independence.

I hope that the above indictment strikes a chord of truth for you. I know it is full of common sense and is based on observable facts. When you step back and look at this country, where it is and where it is headed, do you see any truths here? Remember, my purpose is not to take sides, but to inspire thought based on common sense: a sound judgment based on simple observation of the situation.

The above critiques, according to many modern intellectuals (Noam Chomsky, Thom Hartman, David Korten, Howard Zinn and others), are caused, directly or indirectly, from the development of corporations as we now know them. The crux of the problem is the loss of any social accountability. This one factor has allowed those businesses traded on Wall Street to enforce (with all their political, monetary and physical assets) on *their* definition of growth. Growth for them is not based on any community standards larger than the employment of local workers necessary to meet their goals.

Hear ye! Hear ye!

We hear that several corporations are busy promising to fix the economy with new financial products. Politicians are promising to pass more legislation to protect the environment and the financial marketplace. Institutional religions continue, for over two thousand years, to promise a divine rescue. Schools are working to improve the test scores. New episodes of "Desperate Housewives" and "American Idol" are due out soon to take our minds off the madness!

If you think independently, you have heard or thought this before. But most of us are stuck in our paradigm. We are so stuck that it looks like *it will take an ecological disaster* for people to erase their petty differences and unite against the powers that are destroying this wonderful planet, our home. Perhaps we enjoy our conveniences and entertainment too much to challenge the status quo.

Declarations of Truth

Al Gore declared the environmental decline an "inconvenient truth." I would call the unbalanced economy an "insolvency truth." Our current state of government an "impotency truth." The media deceptions a "propagandic truth." The decline in nutritious food an "unnatural truth."

A "Jeffersonian Truth" as found in the Declaration of Independence is worth our attention:

"whenever any Form of Government becomes destructive of these ends, [life, liberty and the pursuit of happiness] it is the Right of the People to alter or to abolish it, and to institute new Government, laying its foundation on such principles and organizing its powers in such form, as to them shall seem most likely to effect their Safety and Happiness...But when a long train of abuses and usurpations, pursuing invariably the same Object evinces a design to reduce them under absolute Despotism, it is their right, it is their duty, to throw off such Government, and to provide new Guards for their future security..."

Jefferson also wrote,

"Dissent is the highest form of patriotism."

"All tyranny needs to gain a foothold is for people of good conscience to remain silent."

You may recall that the Declaration of Independence includes an impressively long list of grievances against the English crown. It names numerous restrictions, losses of legal process, impositions, refusals and abuses. Our current list of grievances is not yet distilled into a formal declaration but the list is growing among disaffected groups including the owners of failed businesses, the growing homeless and the poor, disillusioned investors and the jobless. We hear their complaints in the underground press, on pirate radio, on the internet, in pulpits, in the polluted rivers, lakes and aquifers, hovering in the urban air, and in the statistics of voter dissatisfaction and citizen apathy.

Time for a Revolution

Thomas Jefferson regarded revolutions as cyclical and necessary. It is still true. The systems we have become so fond of are imperfect. They are also subject to manipulations, abuses and injustice. If that weren't enough, the media that feeds us our information is guilty the same manipulations, abuses and injustices.

Corruption scandals make the press every day. Outside our borders and in our name, the USA has tortured suspects without a trial, bribed and assassinated foreign officials, and used our military to protect American businesses...all this and more without our consent. (Of course it is without our consent; often we are not officially told after the fact.) So, it is time for a change.

While I don't think the government should be let off the hook, the real source of our discontent is the RCMCs. They have taken advantage and control of our democratic, economic and legal processes. The RCMCs use ill-gotten gains and influence to force *our* government's hand. Let's examine the revolution they propose for our planet and home.

Food Revolution

The Resource Controlling Multinational Corporations have made living on this planet completely different from what our grandparents knew just forty years ago. Perhaps food is the most intimate and recognizable change. No longer do we choose from natural, unprocessed foods: grain, vegetables, beans, fruit, dairy, nut and meat products. The bulk of food on the supermarket shelves is packaged and bottled mixtures with added taste and texture enhancements with preservatives and moisture barriers to withstand transportation and delayed consumption.

Row after row of prepared foods dwarf the fresh food offerings. Packaged snacks, mixes, sweetened and alcoholic beverages, dressings, frozen meals and desserts, bottled cleaners and cleaning utensils, disposable babycare products and paper products all make it difficult to leave with just one or two fresh items.

Huge markups with large volume make food production and distribution a highly profitable enterprise. The top ten Wall Street traded food companies (like Nestle, Kraft, PepsiCo, Coca-Cola, Unilever, Tyson, Mars) have captured 35% of the packaged food market[4]. We eat from their selection every day. Their "get rich often" products include cheaply produced candies, chocolate, frozen entrees, soda, ice cream, coffee and snacks. It is pretty hard to understand the force and significance of these foods without looking at some history, but right now, I wanted to focus on the momentum and the likely outcome(s).

> "In the 1970s, the top five beef-packers controlled only about 25% of the market. Today, the top four control more than 80% of the market. Cargill, Swift, Tyson, National Beef. You see the same thing happening now in pork. Smithfield, Swift, Cargill, Tyson."[5]

---

[4],[5] "Food, Inc" documentary

This is largely a result of the demands of the biggest fast food restaurants, the food producers' biggest clients. McDonald's Corporation is currently the largest purchaser of potatoes, and one of the largest purchasers of pork, chicken, tomatoes, lettuce and apples. As a result of this concentration of production, even if we aren't eating in a fast food restaurant we are literally eating foods created for fast food distribution.

We can also expect less food variety in the future, at least from the natural spectrum. Food producers have been playing with the DNA of seeds since 1994 to produce foods that will meet the needs of mass distribution. 93% of soybeans and cotton seed grown in the US are genetically modified. 86% of US corn is genetically modified, according to Wikipedia. Rape seed (for canola oil) and sugar beets are also predominantly (93%) genetically modified in the US[6]. (GMO crops are outlawed in Europe and I think rightly so.)

Our diet in general is significantly less healthy than it was thirty years ago, but not primarily because of recent advances in genetic research. T. Colin Campbell has brilliantly argued in <u>The China Study</u> that our current

---

[6] Wikipedia entry: http://en.wikipedia.org/wiki/Genetically_modified_food

patterns of excess meat consumption and lack of a plant-based diet are the chief causes of modern plagues such as cancer, diabetes, heart disease and obesity. While there are many diet studies and claims, I have to side with The China Study[7] (as does the New York Times[8]) because it is the most exhaustive and most conclusive of any so far. Not only does Dr. Campbell come from a farming background and have impeccable credentials, he studied and observed this study for a full twenty years. To his credit, he avoided producer bias and tells the true story of Washington DC inner workings that have shaped our national diet. If we do not pay attention to the best information about our food sources and how they work in the human body, we can expect to have higher health care costs, more personal health crises, and less life enjoyment.

"Green" Fuel Revolution

With the realization of "peak oil," combined with the need to fuel the growing demand for vehicles and industry, Archer Daniels Midland, BP, Shell, GM, Chevron, DuPont and

---

[7] The China Study by T. Colin Campbell. www.TheChinaStudy.com
[8] The New York Times called The China Study the "Grand Prix of epidemiology" and "the most comprehensive large study ever taken of the relationship between diet and the risk of developing disease."

ConocoPhillips have made major investments to begin converting fast growing plant life into sources of carbon.[9] According to the theory, these carbon based lifeforms can be burned instead of fossil fuels. Understand, these are not plans to reduce greenhouse gases, but to find new carbon-based fuels while creating more products for consumption.

Every year we use as much oil as it took Mother Nature three to four million years to create.[10] We are energy addicted. The systems in place require more fuel. But do we need more carbon-based fuels? Is the green fuel revolution (sometimes referred to as the new "sugar economy") better than completely carbon-neutral solar energy? Wind energy? Tidal energy? Geothermal energy? Isn't the green fuel revolution just another excuse for the major players to stay in power without destroying their established client base?

Bioplastics Revolution.

Plastics have been a boon to sterile individual servings from candy bars and milk bottles to medical supplies and the vast array of consumer product packaging. Many of us

---

[9] ETC Group, November 2008 Communique "Who Owns Nature?"

[10] We Live In Two Worlds, Alf Orpen www.youtube.com/watch?v=KzkAkyMu5Kw

consider plastics effective and essential. Their cheap availability makes other choices hard to make. But diminishing oil supplies will challenge the availability and low cost.

Additionally, we know that we have a tremendous burden of waste in the form of plastics. Beyond waste, plastic production introduces millions of tons of toxins annually to our Earthland home. Many communities are struggling under the burden of the waste. The US alone generates enough plastic water bottles each week to circle the globe five times[11].

With plastics a significant part of today's economy around the world, a "solution" being developed is a range of plastics made partly or completely from renewable life forms. This may reduce the amount of our petroleum use, but oil byproducts are clearly implicated with chemical fertilizers, pesticides, transportation and the machinery of bioplastics production. Waste remains an issue with bioplastics as many are not biodegradable or recyclable.

While application of bioplastics seems limited to packaging, expect to see a lot more development of bioplastics as a "green" solution, even if the pileup of waste

---

[11] Annie Leonard, "The Story of Bottled Water." www.storyofstuff.org/bottledwater

continues. As long as plastics are available, our rampant consumerism will not be abated. Many environmental experts fear that the emphasis on recycling and bioplastics will keep people from considering removing plastics from the environment, as that is the only truly healthy option.

> All plastics migrate toxins into whatever they contact at all times. It does not matter if it is water- or oil-based; hot or cold; solid or liquid," states Paul Goettlich, Director of Mindfully.org.

Homeland Security Revolution

The Patriot Act remains in place ten years after the events of September 11, 2001. With it, federal and local governments retain the ability to shoot first and ask questions later in the cause of "national security." The underground press regularly reports abuses of police powers[12] and military powers[13]

A local man's house (an employee of the Sheriff's

---

[12] Go to www.policecrimes.com or youtube.com and search for "police abuse" videos
[13] Go to www.wikileaks.com

department) was raided yesterday by the FBI. One of the residents told me that the house was completely ransacked for hours by at least ten agents as they searched for digital evidence (not weapons). Innocent parties were handcuffed, detained and left to clean up the dumped papers, ripped out drawers and closets. This assault happened to the home of an "accused" man and his housemates, not anyone found guilty.

Enforcement agencies are proliferating beyond public need or supervision,[14] fueled by fears of chaos. Apparently, Federal and State budgets have a soft spot for security. But these threats are less about citizen security, in my opinion, and more about the RCMC's demands for protection of their growing influence.

Because more citizens have arrest records[15], it would be logical to assume that there will be more restrictions coming for travel, employment and other rights. According to the Washington Post, 1600 people per day are recommended by the intelligence community to be put on the Homeland Security terrorist watch list due to "reasonable suspicion." The list has topped one million people, including minor

---

[14]http://www.statesman.com/news/content/region/legislature/stories/2009/08/23/0823pe aceofficers.html

[15] Information Please Almanac, 2000, 2009

children and aged grandmothers.

The latest wrinkle reminds me of the Hitler Youth movement. The Hitler Youth were to be the eyes and ears of the SS, paying attention to the various activities in their neighborhoods and then reporting on their neighbors, family and friends. A new version has cropped up as a multilevel marketing business opportunity.

The call has gone out for American citizens to report on their neighbors' whereabouts by writing down the visible license plates of parked cars while they go shopping, dining or getting a tan. For every license number the "Information Consultants" enter into the database, the more money they make. On the surface, this appears to be about helping law enforcement track stolen vehicles and legitimate lenders find deadbeat owners. Tracking these cars can give the reporter a sense of participation with the "white hats." But what about the tracking the cars of the majority, those that are paying off their loans or own the car outright? They get reported as well...just for going about their daily business. The "Information Consultants" are awarded income bonuses for signing up more independent spies.

Under Homeland Security, our civil rights look more like a memory than a reality. Police actions have taken on an aggressive, military style. The Patriot Act allows civil authorities to take citizens into custody without telling them or their family the legal justifications for such action. If neighbors are also reporting on others' whereabouts...we can see in our time what citizens under despotic rule have endured[16] and what the Founding Fathers were dealing with when they wrote the Declaration of Independence.

Credit Revolution

Less cash and more fraud. Credit card fraud has not stopped our movement from a cash society to one of digitized creation of credit, more susceptible to fraud. But this is just one layer of fraud.

Perhaps most fraudulent is how "real" money (and monetary wealth, by extension) is created. In the US, all money is created by a bank loan. On the federal level, money is created by loans made to the US Government. For this, the Federal Reserve prints "Reserve Notes," indicating it is a loan owed to the Federal Reserve Bank. On a local level, money is created by loans to credit-worthy customers. But this is not money...it is a debt due to be

---

[16] Naomi Wolfe, The End of America.
http://www.snagfilms.com/films/title/the_end_of_america/

paid. Money as we know it is a debt. (I know this is not what we are taught, but if you research the subject, you will find that this is true.)

The second layer of the fraud is our confusion of money with a credit line. Credit can be "spent" but it is, again, a debt that must be repaid. Credit cards, carried by over a hundred million Americans, are "spent" like money even though they have no value beyond a promise to repay. We are a nation in excess credit card debt.[17]

The third layer of fraud is how digitized value is considered an asset. Consider this: only one tenth of the nation's "monetary" wealth is actually represented in real Federal Reserve Notes (dollar bills). Nine tenths of our "money" is digitized and can be switched, moved, or reentered with simple keystrokes. Given the considerable computer hacking skills of some of the best paid criminals, digitized accounting and market investments in the billions, our money supply is very prone to fraud.

Online banking, banking by cell phone and debit card transactions are making digitized banking swifter and easily accessible to hundreds of millions of people, including hackers. Stolen credit card numbers are so plentiful on the

---

[17] "The Secret History of the Credit Card" www.pbs.org/wgbh/pages/frontline/shows/credit

Internet that they can be purchased in bulk for 1 to 30 dollars each. Is it just that there are millions of digital thieves willing to make a quick sale through their computer and security savvy (and fewer buyers that don't have the hacking ability) or is there an inherent problem with this medium of exchange? If fraud is inherent in the system, why do its creators prefer to sell us fraud insurance instead of designing a safer and more reliable system?

I am all for faster moving information. We need it. But hold onto your hats for even more digitized money "solutions" that are in the banker's interests and not in ours.

Revolution against the poor

The division between rich and poor has been brutal for those on the bottom of the ladder. Worse yet for the overall economy are the millions of middle income people losing jobs, health benefits and their homes, desperately accepting low wage jobs to hold onto the last vestiges of respectability. All the while, the income for the wealthiest continues to climb. Recent figures are stating in no uncertain terms that our present recession displays the biggest spread between rich and poor since just before the Great Depression.

The ratio of salaries of the highest paid employees compared to the average is now 300 to 1 and the highest compared to the lowest is 800 to 1. Compare that to just thirty years ago. Compensation for CEOs of Fortune 500 companies in 1980, compared to the average workers wages, was 42 to 1.[18]

The reason for this inequity seems to have some basis in the tax code. Board members' compensation can be deducted as "business expense" and actually reduce the corporation's tax burden. In effect, the burden of our country's taxes gets shifted to average middle class citizens that have the fewest tax breaks.

Clearly, moral imperatives against this gap are impotent in our current business climate. If legislation does not work to reduce the income gap and require multinational corporations to pay their fair share, the income gap will get worse. Wages in 2007 (the most recent available), gave the top 10% of income earners 49.7% of total US income earned. And the gap widens. During the economic expansion of 2002 to 2007, the top 1% of wage earners captured 2/3's of income growth.[19]

---

[18]   Extreme Inequality.org www.extremeinequality.org/?p=14
[19]   The Huffington Post www.huffingtonpost.com/2009/08/14/income-

The income gap in the US is the biggest gap in any developed nation. If that weren't cause for alarm, where is the common sense that two thirds of the largest corporations in the US paid NO taxes in 2009?[20] Who is left to pay the nation's debts?

Propaganda Revolution

Propaganda uses several techniques to twist the thinking of hearers and readers, using repetition, diversionary "logic," emotional cues and distortion of facts. We are especially susceptible to propaganda when we are confused, not applying critical thinking or not asking tough questions. Some techniques are more subtle and the RCMCs pay big salaries to social scientists to discover how to more easily get past our buying barriers and common sense.

Some examples include news coverage with shorter stories with less facts, more use of bold headlines that appear as complete stories, more compelling imagery created by the best graphic designers and more splashes of color in newsprint. Techniques like sappy male/female news

---

inequality-is-at-a_n_259516.html
[20] Bernie Sanders, The Speech, copyright 2010

anchors seem to satisfy a need for a human connection. Propaganda includes scandal reportage a la Fox News, reportage staffed and funded by corporations and less investigative reporting.[21] Headlines typically announce more predictions of collapsing systems and....News Flash: endless unsubstantiated claims of being "green" and other appropriated emotional fad phrasing.

Though not technically propaganda, the common tactic of omitting facts, relevant context and preceding events can be as powerful as propaganda. Expect more of this from official sources.

Company Owned Everything

Do you remember the history of the company town? This is our future as long as corporations pursue only at the profit motive. At their worst, these towns offered jobs to needy workers but all the service and product prices were fixed so that every paycheck was fully spent for necessities. Company towns usually owned the entire enterprise from housing to grocery stores, gas stations and clothing. In some of the worst cases, employees were not paid in cash,

---

21   Monsanto kills Fox News story about RGBH
       http://www.youtube.com/watch?v=JL1pKlnhvg0

but in vouchers called scrip. Scrip was honored only at company owned stores.

Company towns have been built for lumbering, drilling, mining, steel mills, factory and large engineering projects. By creating the infrastructure, company town owners have felt the right to reap every possible economic benefit. Once the operation is over, such as ending a mining operation, the company withdraws, economically devastating the workforce and their families.

One of the first company towns was Pullman, just outside Chicago in the 1880's. Employees were required to reside in Pullman even though cheaper housing was available elsewhere. The idea is not dead by any means; modern versions exist today. Large, isolated towns created by developers such as Lake Havasu City, AZ and Fountain Hills, AZ began as large blocks of real estate where the developer controlled the development, pricing and industries (the major one being real estate). Walt Disney has created one of the most recent versions in Celebration, Florida.

Today, company towns are a global tactic where the company establishes the living conditions and the rules. They also learn what people are willing to do and what liberties they are willing to give up for employment.

Resource Controlling Multinational Corporations have historically flourished on a worldwide scale, "employing" slaves, servants, child labor and other underpaid help while dominating resources. Wal-Mart, as a modern example, is the world's largest employer. It depends heavily on part time employees to avoid providing health benefits, vacation and profit sharing.[22]

It's a very tidy repeating cycle. Create jobs → Hire for low wages → Induce employee purchases → Invest profits to create more jobs → Hire for low wages, etc. Over time, this creates more low wage earners and when the RCMC grows large enough, it depresses the job market throughout the community. Even the community professionals find their client base dropping and repeat sales diminishing due to the lower living wages.

In 1946, Merle Travis wrote the song "Sixteen Tons" as an ode to the company town.

> *Some people say a man is made outta mud*
> *A poor man's made outta muscle and blood*
> *Muscle and blood and skin and bones*

---

[22]   www.walmartwatch.com

The Entrepreneur That Could   *Casey Jurado*

A mind that's a-weak and a back that's strong

You load sixteen tons, what do you get
Another day older and deeper in debt
Saint Peter don't you call me 'cause I can't go
I owe my soul to the company store

I was born one mornin' when the sun didn't shine
I picked up my shovel and I walked to the mine
I loaded sixteen tons of number nine coal
And the straw boss said "Well, a-bless my soul"

You load sixteen tons, what do you get
Another day older and deeper in debt
Saint Peter don't you call me 'cause I can't go
I owe my soul to the company store

If you see me comin', better step aside
A lotta men didn't, a lotta men died
One fist of iron, the other of steel
If the right one don't a-get you
Then the left one will

60

> *You load sixteen tons, what do you get*
> *Another day older and deeper in debt*
> *Saint Peter don't you call me 'cause I can't go*
> *I owe my soul to the company store.*[23]

I do not intend to indict all corporations here. Many are local, conscientious and make an effort to be responsible community members. I realize that not all corporations are greed driven, war causing, environmentally degrading resource grabbers. What I am opposing is a business model that grows by virtue of greed, dishonesty, influence peddling, unchecked growth and lack of accountability.

Signers of the Declaration

Is the RCMC movement the one you wish to join? It *is* the effort we are currently funding with our taxes, our purchases... and our silence.

Remember the words of Thomas Jefferson, author of the Declaration of Independence,

> *"Dissent is the highest form of patriotism."*

---

[23] Lyrics from www.cowboylyrics.com

"All tyranny needs to gain a foothold is for people of good conscience to remain silent."

Are you ready to sign the Declaration of Independence from the RCMCs? (More on that in section 7.) You know, don't you, that it could cost you all that you have gained under our present false sense of security?

Our Founding Fathers recognized the risk back then. Benjamin Rush, one of the signers of the original document, has been quoted as overhearing a comment between two other signers on July 4, 1776 after the final revision to the document. Benjamin Harrison of Virginia half-jokingly remarked to Elbridge Gerry of Massachusetts, "I shall have a great advantage over you, Mr. Gerry, when we are all hung for what we are now doing. From the size and weight of my body I shall die in a few minutes, but from the lightness of your body you will dance in the air an hour or two before you are dead." Rush remembered that Mr. Gerry "procured a transient smile, but it was soon succeeded by the solemnity with which the whole business was conducted."[24]

---

[24]   The Spur of Fame: Dialogues of John Adams and Benjamin Rush, 1805-1813, John A. Schutz and Douglass Adair, eds.

It is anyone's guess how long the RCMCs can continue to hold this socially, economically and ecologically misguided ship afloat.

I don't believe that the thinking that got us here can extract us.

I do understand that it is insanity to keep doing the same thing over and over while expecting different results.

I also stand sure that the longer the revolution is delayed, the harder and more costly the recovery will be. The Revolution of Common Sense Economics is overdue.

Remember that signing the Declaration of Independence did not create a nation, only the duty to fight for it. For at least forty years after the Revolutionary War, monetary policies were haggled, duels were waged, federal limits and state responsibilities were enacted as interstate commerce issues were negotiated. The Declaration of Independence from the RCMCs is only the first step, but it precedes all progress.

Niche Market Revolution.

During the revolution toward fiscal responsibility and self reliance, niche markets are the most promising opportunities. The beauty of niche markets is their position.

Alert entrepreneurs notice market changes and are flexible enough to retool or start up with low overhead. As the niche business succeeds and grows, it becomes marketable and more profitable than its current annual gross revenue. Niche opportunities typically meet an immediate need the large corporations don't see or don't get involved with early. These human and business needs create niche markets that open up "out of nowhere" and within a few years can take the market by storm.

Examples may include:

- Online auctions and stores serving special interests
- Website development for niche markets
- Document shredding, document security and management
- Translation services
- Small business consultation
- Affordable health alternatives
- Alternative housing
- Pick up and delivery
- Care of senior citizens
- Health advocacy
- Consulting businesses through the maze of governmental regulations

- Supplying the growing demand for medical marijuana
- Whole and specialty foods
- Computer and cell phone applications

As these niche market businesses become profitable, the cycle continues with either competition from the RCMCs or attempts at buying up the market. This is when the smart entrepreneur, without greed, sells for a large profit. This income will provide enough capital for a few to several years as new market opportunities develop. Further examples of these industries are found in section 7, the Niche Market Supplement and will be posted on our website by actual business owners.

Revolution or Devolution?

Will it take the "mother of all disasters" to snap Americans out of our complacency and begin the overdue revolution?

Will we remain so stuck in our comfort zones that when the devolution happens it will be as if all hell has broken loose?

What would the Founding Fathers do?

The next section will begin your training of a revolutionary

ETC mindset. A smart entrepreneur needs common sense, a smarter angle on success and a personal philosophy of money devoid of false economics.

Section Two Summary: Where is the momentum going? More pollution, higher gas prices, less substance and fewer civil rights? The Founding Fathers help us redirect the momentum with common sense and belief in their inspired vision. Several new revolutions are poised for our future, whether we involve ourselves or not. The food revolution will be growing increasingly foreign to the natural landscape and with less variety. Plastics and fuels will be re-engineered by the same producers of the global warming trend. Credit fraud will go unstopped and the ranks of the poor will absorb more of the middle class, as the RCMCs take control of the world town by town. Will you take the step of declaring your independence from them before your town or industry is taken captive? Niche markets are the hope of entrepreneurs as long as the RCMCs miss the opportunities there.

Possessions, outward success, publicity, luxury- to me, these have always been contemptible. I believe that a simple and unassuming manner of life is best for everyone, best both for the body and the mind. – Albert Einstein, scientist, philosopher

Section 3, The ETC Philosophy of Success

Success is simple: knowing what you want and getting it as often as you want. - Mike Renneker

So far, we have looked at where we are as a nation and where we are going. As you already knew, but maybe not in the exact terms I have used, we are in a crisis. Now, let's talk about how we turn this around using common sense, a smart philosophy of money and a better concept of success.

Common Sense

Webster's online dictionary defines common sense in the

clearest way: "sound judgment based on simple observation of the situation or facts." Based on this definition we need two things: sound judgment and simple observation.

Simple observation needs time and attentiveness. Sound judgment needs complete information, that is to say, more than just the interested party's opinions. Sound judgment comes from simple, unbiased observation.

Unfortunately, we have become so unaccustomed to common sense, that we hardly understand how simple and accessible it is. In some cases it is easier to see where it is not.

Obituary for Common Sense

Today we mourn the passing of a beloved old friend, Common Sense, who has been with and served us selflessly for generations. No one knows for sure how old he was, since he seemed to have been always around.

He will be remembered as having cultivated such valuable lessons as: knowing to come in out of the rain; plain speech is best; honesty is the best policy;

don't pour money down a rat hole; the early bird gets the worm; never trust a fool's promise; life isn't always fair; pick your battles; there is no such thing as a free lunch; look before you cross the street; don't trust showmen and carnival barkers.

Common Sense lived by simple, sound financial policies such as "don't spend more than you earn" and "put away for a rainy day," as well as reliable strategies such as, "say please and thank you," "treat elders with respect," "don't say something you will regret later," "don't tell secrets," "gossip doesn't help anything," "ask permission instead of forgiveness," "make peace with your enemies early" and "don't leave large decisions to minors and incompetents."

His health began to deteriorate rapidly when well-intentioned but overbearing regulations were set in place, when complex contracts devoid of common language became the norm, when school policies made administration more important than education, when contracts proliferated in which signers were required to waive their rights to sue the other party for any reason, when laws were created so complex that lawyers became the chief beneficiaries.

Common Sense lost significant weight when prescription drugs proven to have serious side effects, such as causing suicide and heart attacks, were approved by the FDA and allowed to be marketed, when unknown foods were sold by brand recognition and delectable pictures rather than by nutritional value, when diets became more popular than family mealtimes, and when doctors made more money by keeping people getting sick than by educating about health and making them well.

His condition worsened when multinational corporations, headquartered in the US, but not held to US law, acted with the same rights as living persons under the United States Constitution.

Common Sense lost the will to live as the government decided that propaganda was more important than health and education, churches became businesses, and citizens were harassed because they dared to think for themselves.

Common Sense despaired of humanity after a woman failed to realize that a steaming cup of coffee was hot, and after spilling a little in her lap, was awarded a huge settlement; and on recognition that the most watched TV Show of all time was the trial of OJ Simpson and "The Worst TV Show Ever," The Jerry Springer Show, ran for 18 seasons.

Common Sense was preceded in death by his parents, Truth and Compassion; his wife, Discretion; his daughter, Virtue; his son, Reason; and cousins Frugality, Self Reliance, Nutrition and Integrity.

He is survived by his 3 stepbrothers: "I Know My Rights," "It's Not My Fault" and "I Just Work Here."

Because so few realized his value or devotion, funeral attendance was lower than the attendance at the birth of Jesus.

Why is common sense so rare these days? Because it is missing in the these areas where it is essential:

- Our educational system does not teach common sense.
- The media, institutional religion and other authorities discourage questioning their conclusions.
- We have lost our connection with the simple truths observable in nature.
- We are rushed and ceaselessly multitasking instead of reflecting on or observing our situation.

Let's return to the definition of common sense. "Sound judgment based on simple observation of the situation or facts." And let's add one more element. Sound judgment based on simple observation of the situation or facts *moment to moment*. I don't want to complicate the simplicity of common sense, but what good is common sense if it isn't done consistently? What good is common sense if used only when it suits our mood, fits our pocketbook or agrees with our friends? Common sense has to be a way of life if it to work.

> How many legs does a dog have if you call his tail a leg?
> Four. Calling a tail a leg doesn't make it a leg.
> -Abe Lincoln

Growing up in a rural town, I saw common sense in action observing and doing what worked, moment to moment. To improve the learning curve, neighbors listened to what worked for others. Common sense taught them to get along with nature and their neighbors in every way possible. While it made sense to avoid entanglements with the law, farmers expected the laws of the land to be based on common sense.

A successful farmer was one that studied to have enough general knowledge about his/her farming operations that he/she could do all general operations. Building a fence. Tractor repair/oxen yoking. Barn/ house/ shed building and repair. Plumbing and basic electrical wiring. Care and feeding of livestock. Irrigation management, etc. This gave the farmer the ability to oversee the hired help and direct the work when neighbors pitched in. She or he was self reliant.

Today's "Entrepreneurs That Could" need a similar common sense approach: to be self reliant with the new array of tools and technologies that allow him or her to profit in today's economy and shifting business cycles.

What works	What doesn't work
Wearing fewer hats so that important things get done on time.	Habitually spending money on entertainment to reward yourself after a stressful day or week.
Learning the tools of money, business and technology.	Being too busy to find out what is going on around you.
Working with natural	Pursuing dreams without

business and life cycles.	enough financial backing.
Using tax laws and loopholes to improve profitability.	Blaming others for the situation you're in.
Hiring specialists to do their thing so you can focus on yours and receive a better return.	Insisting on doing it all yourself.
Listening to your gut and self justifications.	Accepting others' influences as fact or wisdom.
Looking outside your culture's biases.	Uncritically accepting your own cognitive biases.

A Smart Philosophy of Money

To understand money we need a philosophy. We need to ask what it is. What about money works for us and what doesn't? How much do we need? What is a little money and what is a lot? (There is freedom in both: having a little and a lot !) Is it okay that money runs our lives?

Money, as widely discussed and debated, is not a hard science. It can't be a science because it behaves according to our beliefs about it. Mostly, we believe that money can buy us those things, situations and people that will make us happy. A house. Good health. Comforts. Friendships. Connections. Security. Indulgent things that might make others envious. We believe making more is always better and that pursuing it is sensible. Almost all of us entertain dreams of what we would do if we had more of it.

I know plenty of people with money and I can attest to its advantages:

- access to influence (and associated egotists)[25],
- immunity from the law (if you are inclined to break it),
- added time (by hiring cheap labor to do your labor intensive chores),
- freedom to make more choices (and mistakes),
- added safety (if applied),
- education (but not necessarily wisdom),
- extra medical attention (but not the same as healing or care) and
- toys to please any whim.

If money is able to make us happy for the moment, money is also ultimately impotent against

---

[25]   The parenthetical comments are not intended to be derogatory concerning great wealth, but to identify some limitations of such abundance.

- disease,
- disappointment,
- heartache,
- ignorance (which is different from being uneducated),
- sabotage,
- envy and
- accidents.

No, an abundance of money has not saved the trust fund babies I know from being victimized by and slaves to wasteful living and complete self-destruction. I love the way comedian Groucho Marx sums it up, "Money will not make you happy and happy will not make you money."

Stewardship

The ETC philosophy about money is funded in good stewardship of all resources whether there is a little in your possession or a lot. Also called frugality, stewardship is a mental discipline required to be rich in any resources. Stewardship is wise whether we are rich or poor in knowledge, power, communication, health, sex or relationships. (More on frugality in Section Four.)

What philosophers debate is this: what makes money

valuable? Is it how we spend it? Invest it? Share it? Is it valuable because there isn't enough? Does it buy things because the shopkeeper has to show a profit? Does it have more value in our mattress or the bank account? Specifically, how does it work for me? How does it increase? How much should I keep for emergencies?

My experience has been that money is a better teacher and muse than it is an asset. By teaching me the value of time and things, I learn more by understanding it than having it.

> When I get a little money, I buy books;
> if any is left I buy food and clothes.
> -Erasmus

How much do you need?

The more practical question is this: how much do you need? How much you need may not be what you think. You may be much happier with less instead of more.

Recently, I read about an entrepreneur (Jay Shafer of the Tumbleweed Tiny House Company) that decided that his major living expense, a house, kept him from doing what was most important to him, serving others. So he asked himself if he really needed that house and what he could do as an alternative. He ended up getting rid of his house and building one on wheels. It cost him about $17,000. It eliminated property taxes and his consumerist leanings. True, it is only 960 square feet, but what he wanted most was to serve others, not sit in his house. Now, ten years later, he is still at his happiest, building small houses for others that understand the joys of being with others.

Vicki Robin and Joe Dominguez (now deceased) wrote "the book" on determining how much money you really need. They titled it <u>Your Money or Your Life</u> and it has changed the lives of tens of thousands using nine specific steps toward financial independence. As times have changed since its original publication, Vicki has kept it up to date, still teaching and advocating for a rational and proven approach to money. Even people frightened of money issues have mastered the simple program and learned how much money they really need to live. Once that discovery is made, life and work become partners instead of competitors. What a concept!

But let's not make this complicated. The solution is simple. Money has no consciousness; it depends on our consciousness, for better or worse. When we respect the effort and resources it represents, we know how to use it for the best of all concerned.

How much money you need must be part of your consciousness. What are your real fixed expenses? How much does it cost you to work? To live where you do? To raise and educate your children? To eat healthfully? To recreate? To grow? To clean and clothe yourself? To use a car or other transportation? To save for bigger goals? The answers require you to take an inventory of your own situation.

You probably need a lot less than you think. Henry David Thoreau's comments on simplicity as found in <u>Walden</u>[26] are transforming. His experiment with living a simpler life taught him immense common sense that he generously shared with others in his book. "Simplicity, simplicity, simplicity" fused with his consciousness. If you listen closely, you can also hear "contentment, contentment, contentment."

Believe me, you are more able, inventive and adaptable than you know. You are strong and competent. You will thrive if you are working with the truth. There is no question

---

[26]   Available at libraries everywhere and online for free.
http://thoreau.eserver.org/walden00.html, http://www.gutenberg.org/etext/205

in my mind about that.

But understanding money's true meaning requires that we get out of the mindset created for us by the powerful drivers of the economy. They want us to think that we need more, more, more. They tell us to be dissatisfied with who we are today. They get more out of us when we have a slew of monetary obligations that leave us dead broke. That false and engineered consciousness is at the crux of our environmental, business, personal and political crises.

Choose to be free by discovering how much money you really need and how much you want to share. As you become the master of your money you will become the master of your future.

A word about risk

Investment is an important aspect of money. Where? How often? How much risk is acceptable? Warren Buffett, considered the richest investor alive today, has a principle I think should be passed on. When investing, he just makes sure he never loses.

Losing hard earned money has never been of interest to me, and Wall Street is perhaps one of the biggest cons ever foisted on our economy. It was started by speculators with enough money to lose and is now the preferred place for investments that we can't afford to lose, such as pension plans, college funds, annuities, mortgages and more. (More on Wall Street in section six.)

Money, money, money is not the holy Trinity. Money is a teacher of risk and obligation and one part of a common sense way to be self-reliant. Here are a few more quick suggestions.

- Read more on our website. www.TheEntrepreneurThatCould.com
- Search for answers that come from wise and money-smart entrepreneurs you know.
- Stop thinking, "I don't have enough."
- Get past any shame regarding your present money status. It is only temporary, especially if you follow the examples of money savvy entrepreneurs I will introduce to you in later chapters.

Finally, don't confuse having a lot of money with "wealth." You may know the Navaho definition of wealth. Like them, I believe that real wealth is being one who is respected, whose opinion is sought and who has enough to share. The real measure of a person is not monetary wealth or material possessions; it's wisdom and knowledge and one's ability to contribute to society as a whole. That is wealth and success.

ETC Success

Culturally in America, success is the same as wealth and high profitability. I have no doubts that the Ted Turners, Lee Iacoccas, Martha Stewarts and Donald Trumps think of themselves as successful. So, what about you? How do you measure your success? Is it based on

- Money?
- Life accomplishment?
- Attractiveness?
- Day by day goals?

Is it measured by

- Sticking to your principles?
- Service?
- Doing good?
- Health?
- Learned wisdom?
- Comforts?
- Ease?
- Children?

- Contribution?

If you died without leaving behind some significant amount of money and assets, could you say that your life was a successful one? Why or why not?

The reality today is that a large percentage of us will die without leaving behind a large estate. There are less than 7.5 million millionaires (exclusive of home valuation) in the US. That is roughly 3% of the population. The rest of us (97%) will probably either outlive our income or leave debt behind for our heirs. Not only do we live longer and spend more, our pensions and savings are not making the kind of money we were promised. Lifetime savings are being pulled out of investment portfolios at an alarming rate just to survive the most recent, engineered economic cycle. Our health care expenses have skyrocketed, even threatening some of the millionaires. Our economy feels unstable and its cycles are forcing more into foreclosures and homelessness. Will a life well-lived be eclipsed by a ledger sheet?

Success from a common sense perspective means that it doesn't take a profit line or an MBA to have success. Think of great leaders, inspirational writers and philosophers from the past. They had success but how many of them died millionaires?

- Thomas Jefferson spent most of his life plagued by crushing debt. (But not from foolishness or a poor grasp of economics. His priority was science, developing educational institutions and creating history.)

- Judy Garland, the popular star and singer was so indebt that it took her daughter's success (Liza Minnelli) to raise money for a proper burial.

- Sammy Davis, Jr. died penniless, owing millions in taxes.

- Jesus Christ and the Buddha died homeless and without leaving behind a single written word.

Success comes from criteria other than personal wealth.

Success on the broad scale is really about inquiry, integrity and common sense. A successful mother, father or teacher is a high calling, a calling missed by the world's most asset-rich. Do you realize how successful a smile is? An encouraging word? A helping hand? Remember the quote at the beginning of this chapter by Mike Renneker. "Success is simple: knowing what you want and getting it as often as you want it."

Contemplate a few quotes of rare sense penned by Henry David Thoreau. They are well worth the paper they are printed on!

- "I know of no more encouraging fact than the unquestionable ability of man to elevate his life by a conscious endeavor."

- "Most of the luxuries and many of the so-called comforts of life are not only not indispensable, but positive hindrances to the elevation of mankind."

- "Rather than love, than money, than fame, give me truth."

- "To be a philosopher is not merely to have subtle thoughts, nor even to found a school, but so to love wisdom as to live according to its dictates, a life of simplicity, independence, magnanimity, and trust."

The ETC Philosophy gives an entirely different perspective from the dominant paradigm. The paradigm we all know is that we are consumers, doing our part by paying our large mortgage and driving to a job every day to work harder than any other westernized citizen while keeping our lawns trim and green and making sure our children get the best education we can afford. This ideal is based on money, not value and misses out on the real joys and successes of life.

Acknowledging this is to take the first step toward ridding ourselves of the confusion. In the next section, we will look at the qualities of character that make your success a sure thing: the disciplines of frugality, self reliance, nutrition and integrity.

Section Three Summary: Common Sense has been on vacation for so long that rumors circle about "his" death. Common sense is best defined as sound judgment based on simple observations of the situation but we hardly know to come in out of the RCMC reign. Common sense observes from moment to moment what works and what doesn't.

Common sense often disappears when it comes to money and success. Money can   promise the fulfillment of dreams but it merely encourages happiness; it does not guarantee it. If we want more happiness, we can get that better from understanding money than having it. Money is the great teacher of stewardship, a necessary skill applicable to all resources. ETC success understands the local Bank of Resources has more than money we can withdraw.

*First they ignore you, then they laugh at you, then they fight you,
then you win. – Mahatma Gandhi, founder of modern India*

Section 4, The Disciplines of ETC

*To be without some of the things you want is an
indispensable part of happiness. -Bertrand Russell*

In Section 3, it was my intent to share foundational
philosophies I have learned from successful entrepreneurs.
But when you are running a business, disciplines will also
be required. These disciplines, though the word sounds
unpleasant, are proven methods to keep your business and
your life on track. Disciplines are not worse than the
alternative, by the way. The alternative to being guided by
disciplines is like feeling your way around a desert,
confused by the unremarkable landscape and being eaten

slowly by the harsh realities of the environment. Disciplines, like a simple compass in strange territory, can save you lots of grief.

In this section, the Four Directions of the compass are cousins of Common Sense: Frugality, Self Reliance, Nutrition and Integrity. This Compass of Possibility has the four directions coming to a center point, right here and now. The compass will assist you in moving forward, but only if you use it.

Frugality

Whether your resources are plenty or sparse, good stewardship is just plain common sense. Another word for this stewardship is frugality. Frugality is a mental discipline that helps maximize any resource, whether it is personal health, money, relationships, knowledge, power, communication or shared community assets.

Frugality is sometimes confused with being stingy. Stinginess has no part of being a smart entrepreneur. Stinginess is like grabbing the money in your pocket and refusing to invest it, give in gratitude or spend to please a partner. Stinginess is reactive. Stinginess looks for a payout without adequate investment (something for nothing). It refuses to invest in one's future. It gives only with reserve and has an underlying resentment for the responsibilities associated with money.

Frugality, on the other hand, is a type of wisdom. It has a respect for how a resource works and knows its true value. It understands that all resources are limited, as is life itself. Frugality is a conscious partnership that makes the discipline an honor to exercise.

Frugal examples

Take the example of frugality with money. The frugal person understands the money that was spent on him or her as a child as a representation of years of hardship borne by one's parents; earned money is a result of personally invested hours of education and training; money is the result of time and effort by applied labor in a specific money-friendly environment. Then, after spending certain hours of time and effort, a frugal person also recognizes that the asset called money can leave their wallet or purse in less than a half of a minute. In most cases, the asset will not be returned. Now spent, a new expenditure in time, resources and effort will be required to replace it.

Frugality of the resource we call "time" recognizes that time is limited and is impossible to retrieve. What is time worth in terms of what we can trade for it? Should it be spent on indulgent pleasures or procrastination without due consideration for the return in the coin of happiness, accomplishment, knowledge or contribution?

Money and time are essential assets that can be drained in multiple ways. Do you know anyone that spent 30 years on a bad marriage? Or spent 20 years being kicked around by a disrespectful office manager? Or went around the world looking for the answers to life when the answers were inside them all along? Or threw away a good education for drinking and partying? We have many assets to waste, conserve or spend wisely with a frugal consciousness.

Borrowing money is particularly painful for the frugal. This ill-advised risk ignores that we are very inaccurate predictors of the future, particularly our financial future. Especially when money is tight, it is not a time to act as if we have more than we do. It is time to get creative and to be driven to new solutions that could also help other people in similar circumstances. An example is The Tightwad Gazette written by Amy Dacyczyn. In her quest for a frugal lifestyle, she found ways to help others learn the ropes.

I recall a friend of mine that went through some really tough financial times. He and his wife knuckled down and stayed with a frugal life style. Eventually, they became very wealthy. But what is helpful to notice is that whether times were good or hard, he was the first one to volunteer to buy the 12 pack every Friday night for his friends. He was frugal enough to feed his family and share with his friends at the end of the work week. Frugality is a disciplined partnership that maximizes the asset's potential for all concerned.

What Would Ben Do?

Ben Franklin has been an inspiration to entrepreneurs the world over. His publication of "Poor Richard's Almanack" was full of timeless nature-wise and humorous advice for getting the most out of life in America. It was a best seller for twenty six years. Frugality was a keynote of Ben's. Though he is credited with the saying, "A penny saved is a penny earned," he also advised against wasting time. "If time be of all things the most precious, wasting time must be the greatest prodigality." "Time is money" was penned by Ben.

Thomas Jefferson believed that good government ought to be frugal, and avoid taxing the citizen's labor or the bread that the laborer earned. "A wise and frugal government, which shall restrain men from injuring one another, shall leave them otherwise free to regulate their own pursuits of industry and improvement, and shall not take from the mouth of labor and bread it has earned. This is the sum of good government."

Frugality makes Self Reliance possible

Self Reliance is not taught in school. We may have been taught some wilderness survival skills in one of the various scouting programs, but self reliance is not survival, it is a lifestyle.

Self reliance was the goal of the new American nation as it broke free from England's controlling grasp. That meant more than self governance. It meant economic self sufficiency, trading partnerships, cohesive monetary policies, and resource allocation. Everyone was expected to pitch in and make allowances for getting others up to speed. Without self sufficiency, they would lose their hard won freedom and become slaves to new owners.

The emerging nation had bills to pay for the war, fund the creation of the Federal Government and markets to forge to bring in foreign money and investment. It was a young nation, fortunately made up mostly of people under twenty years old with ambition and determination. Even with this advantage, if they had foolishly squandered their resources, the nation would not have stood. Frugality was their ticket.

What are your assets for Self-Reliance?

Anyone with common sense knows that before they start a project, one must consider their assets. What are they and are they sufficient to complete the task?

I had an economics professor that asked his class, "What is a person's most important asset?" The students had the typical answers you'd expect: their investment portfolio, their home, their retirement account, their home equity, their inheritance. "It's none of those," the professor explained. "Your most important asset is the ability to earn an income. Whatever that may be. It may be plowing a field and harvesting it. Or you may be an artist and able to sell enough work to sustain you...whatever you are capable of doing." The professor proved his point by asking us what we thought would happen to us when our ability to make an income disappeared. This lesson has stuck with me ever since.

What if a recession hit and you were laid off? You may have a disabling accident or disease. A new technology could put you out of work. A family crisis may keep you from being productive. What happens when you lose your best asset? You are no longer self-reliant. You must depend on an insurance payout, relatives or you might become a ward of the state.

There are many elements of self-reliance. Creativity. Knowledge. Persistence. Courage. Generosity. Innovation. Optimism. Why are these character traits of self-reliance not taught in our public schools? If we were taught self-reliance, we would be taking responsibility for our future and not leaving it in the hands of politicians and large multinational corporations. We would be happier, I assure you, because we would not live in fear of losing our jobs or pensions. We would be capable of managing our own businesses. If we were self-reliant, we would make up our own minds instead of being swayed by the media. But perhaps the bottom line is that we would not consume at the rate we do or need large doses of credit that are making a few people in the world very, very rich. (We now have more billionaires than ever: 112.)

Vicki Robin and Joe Dominguez, authors of <u>Your Money or Your Life</u>, make a great case for becoming as self-sufficient as possible by taking stock of the asset called "life energy." It is the one real thing we have that we can trade. Readers are asked to consider how many life energy units they have and what are those units buying? Everything we buy or participate in requires life energy. This redefines the cost of everything including health, transportation and dependence on a paycheck.

Shared Reliance

The fuller story about reliance has always been that no one is completely self-reliant. Being self-reliant requires a community of people working and doing what makes the community balanced and locally feasible. Although there is a small minority that are able to eek out an existence in the middle of nowhere, the large majority of us are better adapted to shared reliance.

Look at the way American farmers used to feed, clothe and house their families. They bartered, traded and exchanged for livestock or produce. Neighbors helped with barn-raising and harvests. Farmers lent their tools and planting wisdom to other farmers. Assets were shared.

If Farmer Johnson's son had an accident, like Johnny's legs getting run over by a cart, and amputation was needed, the town would find a way to support Johnny and his family by finding some work he could do without legs. Maybe he could sew leather or fit wood barrel slats together. The town would rally together because Johnny was one of them and he needed to be as self-reliant as they were.

> I have seen that in any great undertaking it is not enough for a man to depend simply upon himself.
> -Isna-La-Wica, Sioux warrior

Today, "horse trading" and bartering are uncommon. We depend on the faceless market to establish a value for products and services, which we dutifully pay with cash or credit. If the store owner's son has an accident, the community might raise funds for Johnny or get him on welfare. This does not help Johnny become self-sufficient. It pays some of his bills. After some months, Johnny is not seen in public anymore as he no longer has the kind of money he needs to participate. He is a dependent. Without community focus, creativity and action that keep us self-reliant, we can easily become burdens on others.

Credit Reliance

Do we value being self-reliant anymore? Not as a society. Today, the system favors consumers who use credit to finance their purchases. This is indebtedness and it runs completely counter to self-reliance. I can't help but recall the words of Founding Father John Adams, "There are two ways to conquer and enslave a nation. One is by the sword. The other is by debt." Thomas Jefferson had a similar mind on the subject, "I believe that banking institutions are more dangerous to our liberties than standing armies." This truth was spoken by a man who knew from personal experience how bad it was to have standing armies in town, and banking institutions posed a worse threat.

Nutrition

Nutrition is one of the most telling of ETC disciplines. It is the ultimate exercise of self-responsibility and self-reliance. I am not saying anyone should do nutrition my way. The degree you take it is up to you. Besides sticking with nutritious food, well-digested on a natural cycle, the key is to keep it simple. Good nutrition is simple.

I am simply amazed by the stunning amount of evidence that what you eat can control and enhance how you feel. It is that simple and that dramatic. The studies show that if you eat right, you can literally avoid cancer and debilities like diabetes. Who doesn't want that? But the way most people eat, it's like playing roulette with their bodies. With longevity up, maybe they will live a long life with good health *and* maybe they will live for many years, held together by painful surgeries and expensive drugs. But if you eat right, a diet of mostly plants with limited animal proteins and sugar, you can feel young for a majority of your last years.

If you are interested in an unbiased, 20 year study, I recommend The China Study by T. Colin Campbell. He was raised on the farm. He knows agriculture. He observed and recorded the longest nutrition study ever conducted. No large corporations funded it, looking to advance some biased results. Remarkably, the results were as clear as any study can be. It is simple, like I said earlier. All good health requires is a diet of mostly plants with limited animal proteins and sugar. Period. These people had vastly fewer occurrences of cancer, diabetes, heart disease and autoimmune disease. The book is thick and a bit laborious, yet a rewarding volume of scientific information. Dr. Campbell also details how politically difficult it is in America to prevent disease with good nutrition.

By the way, don't look to the medical profession for clear information about nutrition and diet. Neither doctors nor nurses are given more than a few hours of education in nutrition and they are taught the outdated food pyramid created by the food distribution industry.

The entire medical community does not want us to know about nutrition. How could that be? Because their very existence is based on people getting sick. People that eat sensibly don't get as sick. Would a doctor want to give their prospects the tools to avoid coming to see them? No, they have expensive loans to pay off, and while there are exceptions, many clearly have a need to display the symbols of power in the community.

The pharmaceutical industry depends on sick people as well. When they get extra greedy, they pay researchers to discover and name new syndromes. In 2010, researchers discovered a new one... "Orthorexia Nervosa." Unlike Anorexia Nervosa, a disorder of not-eating, this is the condition suffered by those that always and only choose healthy food. Seriously. Look it up on the Internet. One "expert" says that always eating healthy can lead to death. (So can breathing the air.)

Conversely, consider those societies that make up the impoverished "Third World." To them meat is a luxury. They eat plants because they can grow them and it is the cheapest way to eat. They are keenly aware how much it costs to raise an animal on grains that could be feeding one of them. (It takes about 10 times the food to raise an animal for slaughter than for a human to eat it directly from the harvest.) And when you study their disease rates... you will see their cancer rates are low, autoimmune disease is low; they don't even know what diabetes is...until they come over here. After three generations of exposure, their health is comparable with the rest of America. That is what our American, RCMC dependent diet does for people that were not predisposed to chronic disease.

I don't think want to shame anyone into nutrition. It is your body and you should do with it what you want. In our system, you are free to smoke cigarettes like a smokestack, develop lung cancer, get a tracheotomy, smoke some more, go on a ventilator, die a slow death in and out of hospitals and convalescent centers, and charge your care to the insurance company that is covering me, too. That is your right.

> I love the colors of plant food. Fruits and vegetables beckon our eye with their bright coloring. Reds, oranges, purples and greens. They are like tiny nuclear reactors. It's miraculous. The tastes are powerful when eaten raw rather than cooked and what it does to the body is more than delicious. The life of a raw food knows exactly what to do inside us. Sometimes the shape of the food gives us a clue as to what it will do for us, like the way the inner tomato mimics the heart muscles, a sliced carrot resembles an eye, a brain-shaped walnut helps cognitive processes and oblong olives help regulate ovulation.

You don't have to be a fanatic, either, growing a ponytail or wearing a tapestry to be conscious of nutrition. It has nothing to do with shaving your legs or armpits. It has to do with understanding who you are as a human being and how you are a part of it. Real food is less expensive, too. It is easier to get and the long term benefits are "up there" with knowledge and wisdom.

I observe that if people are not willing to make a commitment to their health, they are not going to be open to the commitment to other life improvements. I believe nutrition is a singularly important choice for self-reliance. Nutrition is a major test of one's ability to survive, think for one's self (instead of following the herd) and get in touch with our common source.

Integrity

Over the five decades of my life, I think that I have always valued integrity. I wanted it from my parents. I expected integrity with my business partners. I wanted it from my spouse. I needed it from my government.

Sadly, for most of my life, I have been out of integrity. Only recently have I really learned to be honest about that. Please understand as you read this that I am not pointing a finger at anyone, telling them how to be in integrity. We are all on our path and integrity is one of the most important learning tools at our disposal. I would not have an ounce of integrity if I pointed the finger of shame.

> Mahatma Gandhi's advice to "Be the change you want to see in the world" squarely figures with personal integrity.

You may recognize the easiness with which we blame another for our own situation. Learning that each situation is our own, instead of theirs, may be the first lesson in integrity. And this may take a great deal of personal adjustment. Integrity this gritty means the failure of "my" marriage is my doing. (Or at least 50% of it is.) The bankruptcy and the partnership failures as well as my health, my prejudices and my limitations are mine. They are no one else's.

This realization is not to in order to blame myself. It is to empower and understand myself. As I peel back layers of stories and perceptions, I get closer to this truth. I realize that it is me that was blocking myself. It is up to me to change any of it.

Topics, a method of integrity

Several years ago, I wanted to learn to play guitar. The man I hired was a fellow by the name of Mike Renneker. He arrived early on the appointed day while I was having a business discussion with my partner. When Mike came in, I noticed his unkempt appearance. He had scruffy gray hair, well-worn jeans (before torn jeans were fashionable) and his beat up old Toyota truck confirmed my judgment that guitar-playing was all he had going for him. He saw that I was busy and kindly said, "Take your time. I'll be here when you're done."

After I finished my business meeting, I found out that he had been listening in because he asked, "Do you mind me telling you something personal?" I thought he was going to criticize me, but I agreed to hear his assessment. "That discussion you were having with that gentleman...I don't know who he is, but it's never going to work."

I shook off the shock and asked if he minded telling me why he thought it wouldn't work.

That's when he began introducing me to his life philosophy. "I run my life according to a method I call 'Topics.'" He gave me an overview of "Topics," a method he had developed with some friends. After the lesson, Mike offered to have me over at his house for the next lesson. "Same time. Next week."

I wondered who this guy was and who he thought he was. When I arrived at the address, I had more questions. Outside, the house was impressive in style and size. The best explanation seemed to be that he was giving a guitar lesson to the wealthy owner and this was not his house. Inside, artwork covered the walls and books filled the spaces in between. I asked Mike straight out if it was his house and he said it was. The next question was to figure out why a man this wealthy was going around giving guitar lessons.

But Mike wanted to tell me about his group of friends. Together they had developed a method of success they called "Topics." One guy was a plumber. Renneker was an accountant. One was a builder and another, a doctor. They would meet regularly at a ski resort and spend hours discussing important topics. For years their discussion was to hammer down the meaning of success. It ended up being "knowing what you want and getting it as often as you want."

Mike pointed out that this method made it easy to determine clearly if his or anyone else's life was successful.

One simply asks, "do you have what you want and as often as you want?" "Topics" uses the philosophical "tabula rasa" (blank sheet) argued by Rene Descartes. On that blank slate, or blank sheet, he lists his life goals, the "wants."

So instead of a guitar lesson, he sat me on the deck with a yellow pad of paper and told me to write down all the important things I wanted in my life. Those became my "Topics." Once I wrote them down, he instructed me to post those topics on a wall within my mind. "Put them all over. And later, you can pull them down, crumple them up and throw them away."

Then he told me about the discussion with my partner he had overheard. "You were talking about making money. You were here and he was over there. You were so far apart from each other's individual topics that I could sense that it would never work for you. I have seen it a thousand times." I started getting defensive. I thought, "Mike doesn't know me; he doesn't know my partner. What makes him think he can understand where we are coming from?"

As he spoke about "Topics," I learned that the key is to find out where one's own topics (goals/ wants) will not mesh; there the priorities, methods and concepts cancel each other out. Conflicts between topics will keep a person from becoming successful. They indicate lack of functional integrity. By making the life goals conscious, detailed and mentally prominent, every topic can be reevaluated, rewritten and reconstructed.

We had four or five more meetings and I never learned to play the guitar. But I did learn how he made exactly the amount of money he wanted and still had the free time to pursue his passions. He had achieved success through the integrity of knowing exactly what he wanted, topic by topic.[27]

The story of stories

Communication is a great vehicle for making human connections, but we easily use it to tell ourselves and others "stories." Too often, these stories cover up our lack of integrity.

These stories start early in our lives. We create them to get what we need in a world in which we are, at first, helpless. These are stories about dependence on others, how they fail us and how we fail. We aren't even conscious that we are making up these stories, but we keep the ones

---

[27] Read more of Mike's story at www.TheEntrepreneurThatCould.com

that work for a lifetime. They habitually run in the mental background and whenever they don't square with reality, we adjust and temper them to reinforce our earlier perceptions.

Mental stories are inevitable. But do they square up with each other? And do they align with reality? There is no integrity in identifying a problem and not doing anything about it. There is no integrity in failing to care for those that have cared for us. There is no integrity in telling ourselves that our needs are more important than others' needs. And there is no integrity telling ourselves the story that others' needs are more important than ours.

Reality is Integrity is Reality

Integrity is how reality exists. In other words, reality is not at odds with itself. Reality does not lie to itself about what it is. Reality is completely whole and consistent.

What happens when we do not have integrity? What does it mean when we blame society for its lack of integrity when we do not have it? Is there any integrity in blaming society for misleading us, using us, or denying our rights or being unfair? No. Society is made up of individuals and if the component parts are faulty, then the collective cannot be anything but faulty. So, the reason society is screwed up is because each one of us played a part in that. We must own up to our part of the breakdown before we can build a new collective with integrity.

Let's start having integrity with our words.

Years before language became written, the spoken word was a person's promise. To break your word back then was not just an affront to the one you talked to; you offended the entire clan or village. Once the trust was broken, it might take a half of a lifetime to restore it. If however, you acted on your word, there was integrity. My understanding is that American Indians embraced this ethic, too. So when invading Europeans dined with Indians, gave their word and just as promptly acted differently, they deserved the reputation of "white man speaks with forked tongue."

One thing that separates animals from humanity is our ability to communicate with words. We have the words, but we are still stumbling over them. We are clumsy communicating with one another and I think that is because we have not focused on developing integrity behind our words and actions.

You may recall listening to a person of integrity at some point in your life and something within you knew that the words they spoke were as straight as an arrow and as rooted to reality as a stately oak. I understand that kind of integrity is how Nelson Mandela survived his twenty-seven years in prison. On multiple occasions, guards were ordered to go to his cell and kill him; they went to his cell but could not kill him. It was the integrity of his words and presence that made them unable to permanently silence him. Mahatma Gandhi was another rare human with an integrity that stopped his opposition cold. Eventually, after several assassination attempts, a bullet did end his life. But it was too late to stop the message that rang clear with integrity.

Owning our integrity

Today, much of humanity is suffering from the lack of integrity. We lie. We spread lies and half truths to promote our position, our economic style, our religion or our political agendas. The integrity of being human requires realizing that we are no better than anyone else. A higher education never made anyone better any more than skin or eye color could. What's more telling is that we have lost integrity with our environment.

Many primal cultures such as the Native Americans, Maoris, Polynesians and Australian Aboriginals understand that we are all one. They learned this from the sun, moon, oceans, stars and seasons. This integrity with the environment fosters integrity among them. Integrity teaches them that we are all here for the others and that exploitation of any is not an option. The natural cycles teach all of us that each species has its time and its integrity. Examples include, "You don't pick apples before they are ready to fall." "You take only what you can use immediately." "There is enough for all when we don't hoard."

Author Daniel Quinn wrote about integrity with the earth's cycles in the fanciful tale called <u>Ishmael</u>. To summarize, Ishmael, a telepathic gorilla, finds and instructs his human pupil about the two kinds of people on the earth, the Leavers and the Takers. The Leavers understand their place in the cycles of nature. The Takers do not have integrity with their surroundings, creating shortages and wars of expansion.

According to Ishmael, human beings living eons ago dwelt

as clans that were defined by their environment as it yielded their sustenance. The clans would expand and contract based on the fruitfulness of the plants or the migration patterns of animals. Sometimes another clan would come in to raid their food sources. The Takers realized by their raids that they had another option for feeding their growing needs. Raiding was their reaction to the feeling of not having enough. And raiding was concentrated on their needs without consideration of others'. The resulting devastation illustrated their lack of integrity.

Most of us were taught that Native Americans lived by a slightly different version. They had an advanced appreciation for sustainability, hunting and gathering by mimicking nature's way of trimming off the herd without decimating it. They also left behind berries, bark and roots for natural replenishment or for starving wanderers. This did not always yield food in plentiful quantities. But their aim was not quantity; it was imitating the integrity they observed around them.

Shared Integrity

What may be more important for us to understand at this

time is that for Leavers or Takers (or any other type of human community), the integrity of the group is dependent upon the integrity of the individual members. Your ability to integrate with others stands on your reputation for being truthful with them and being truthful about who you are. Likewise, those that are held in the highest esteem in any community are usually those whose word is their bond, whose products are of high quality (thus better value) and whose services are genuine. Don Miguel Ruiz makes this point well in his book The Four Agreements, particularly the agreement to "be impeccable with your word."

On a practical level today, imagine our communities with people at every level involved in the health and viability of that community. It would be a community where administrators of cities kept the citizens informed and helped them make the best community decisions. Where children attended council meetings and became part of making the city good for their neighbors. Where firefighters used their extra days off to work with seniors, pick up trash or manage community gardens. Where business owners taught business principles in high school and the grads apprenticed in successful ventures. Where senior citizens had a place to be honored, heard and served. Where neighbors bragged about their superior local resources instead of leaning on the institutions of bigger cities.

Such opportunities are in every neighborhood. Today we have the technology and the resources. We have successful models to learn from. We can make this choice one by one and honor the life we have been given.

Our main asset as humans is to support ourselves within the natural systems we have been given. We can do this now. We are past the point where we need to raid another village or country to feed our children. We can raise every American to self-sufficiency and thereby build a strong core upon which this nation can stand. It would make the Founding Fathers proud.

> *"Resolve to perform what you ought; perform without fail what you resolve." Ben Franklin*

> *"To be prosperous is not to be superior, and should form no barrier between men. Wealth ought not to secure the prosperous the slightest consideration. The only distinctions which should be recognized are those of the soul, of strong principle, of incorruptible integrity, of usefulness, of cultivated intellect, of*

fidelity in seeking the truth." William Ellery Channing

"As I have said, the first thing is to be honest with yourself. You can never have an impact on society if you have not changed yourself... Great peacemakers are all people of integrity, of honesty, but humility."
Nelson Mandela

Section Four Summary: The four cousins of Common Sense are Frugality, Self-reliance, Nutrition and Integrity. Like a compass with four directions, we must start with one, Frugality. Frugality is not stinginess, it is a respect for the value of resources including time, relationships, money and education. Frugality makes Self-reliance possible. Self-reliance requires creativity, knowledge, persistence, courage, generosity, innovation and optimism. This makes Self-reliance perhaps the best builder of American character. It was a shared Self-reliance that grew the colonies into nationhood. Self-reliance requires self care and nutrition is a way we care for ourselves three times a day. Convenience foods fail us and we would be better eating nothing in most cases. In today's nutrition-deprived consciousness, eating healthy requires Integrity. Integrity is the closest of the four disciplines to "True North". Societies depend on it. Nature lives by it. We die for lack of it. I am still learning to be in Integrity and this book is a public statement of moving toward my truth. I trust it rings true for all of my tribe here on this wonderful planet Earth.

The care of the Earth is our most ancient and most worthy, and after all our most pleasing responsibility. To cherish what remains of it and to foster its renewal is our only hope. – Wendell Berry, ecologist, author

Section Five, Nature Rules.

Nature has been accused of being demanding, relentless, challenging, impersonal, harsh and unforgiving. These words are often thrown about after a deluge of weather or other natural disaster. But Nature is also called our Mother, bounteous, inspiring, giving, soothing, sexy, brilliant, home, regenerating, beautiful and abundant. Certainly Nature has also been forgiving if you look at the untold billions of tons of minerals extracted, trillions of miles of soil paved over and billions of buildings erected. Yes, Nature has been forgiving.

But many of us are expecting a disaster on the horizon as an estimated 100 species become extinct each day, climate warming shrinks glaciers and snow caps, new antibiotic-resistant viruses make their debut, genetic mutations become more common and pollinators under-serve our crops.

I am not here to debate global warming, though scientific and simple observations indicate climate change is very real. My point is simple: we are products of Nature and do ourselves harm by failing to maintain integrity with our source.

Natural Science Two Hundred Years Ago

One of my favorite Founding Fathers is Thomas Jefferson. Jefferson was one of the finest minds of his time, not just in the colonies. Much of his fascination lay in natural history. His book "Notes on the State of Virginia" is full of observations about the flora, fauna, mountains, rivers, climate and fossils found in his region. Additionally, he correctly predicted the eclipse of 1778 with great accuracy and made contributions for the improvement of almanacs on the equation of time. Jefferson was considered an expert in anatomy, civil engineering, physics, mechanics, meteorology, architecture, and botany. What a mind!

Another naturalist Founding Father was Ben Franklin, author and publisher of "Poor Richard's Almanack." Besides the wordplay and entertaining proverbs he scribed, colonists used the weather and astronomical information contained in the almanac to plan ahead for planting and seasonal variations.

Ben was an eager student and promoter of natural philosophy, a philosophical approach to the natural sciences. His curiosity about Nature is most often remembered in his experiments to prove that lightning is bursts of electricity. (This led to his invention of the lightning rod, saving many buildings from fire.) Ben was also the first scientist to study and map the Gulf Stream. He measured wind speeds, current speed, depth and temperature. Ben's interest was not simply to catalog natural events; his interest was to find the efficiencies that can make natural laws work on the behalf of human growth and vitality. What an example!

The Empire vs. Nature

Ben and Thomas' interests were science based, yet they were also philosophers, thinking about the meaning of their scientific studies. So pardon me if I get philosophical here. We are living on very small planet. Yes, it is really small. We have to share.

But there has been a monopoly game going on for control of its lands and resources since the rise of the empire state. These resources are enough for our combined benefit, but that is not how it is working out. The limited resources are being manipulated, controlled, hoarded and used in destructive ways. As a single example, the four percent of the world's population that is the United States uses about 50% of the available resources. And we are controlling the search for new resources.

Most of us think of Nature as being outside of us, but the fact that we have reactions to pollutants, pesticides, chemical additives and shelf life extenders is a reminder that Nature is within each of us. It is this lack of connection between "Nature within" and "Nature without" that causes us much confusion. It is a lack of integrity.

These days we are so adapted to this lack of connection that we can hear a news flash about polluted lakes and rivers and not be emotionally affected. We can be told that an ecosystem is fragile and we should not intrude, but we do anyway. We can read that a species of bird, African wildlife, sea coral or ocean bass is in danger of dying out and we continue doing exactly what we were doing before. But whether we know it or not, Nature is inside us, reacting, rejecting foreign particles and allowing the breakdown of minor systems to save major ones.

A Word from the Ancients

Before the history books told the stories of the rise of Western Civilization, the "ancients" related to their source of supply on a symbiotic basis. Today, they have been labeled as "Nature worshipers" or "Pagans." We can't really understand their take on Nature using our typical Westernized institutional religious overlay, but it seems that to them, Nature was less worship and more respect; less obedience and more cooperation; less formality and more inevitable relatedness; less leader-prompted and more community-enacted.

We can tell that they ordered their lives around natural cycles such as solstices, planets, seasons, harvests, river flows and plantings. This connection was so ingrained in ancient humans that when more formalized religions came into power, many of the same markers were incorporated for the new religious holidays. For instance, Christianity's Easter and Christmas are replacements for spring and winter solstice observations.

Today we are observing another incarnation of the

holidays. As western Christianity's cathedrals were built over formerly Pagan sites, this empire is being built on top of the Christian one. The new culture is Consumerism. Holidays that once were celebrated as times of reflection and renewal have been turned into retail splurges. Each of us have our own way of incorporating this shift toward retail purchases into our holiday celebrations, and no matter how religious we are, there is no ignoring the expectation to join in the shopping for clothes, cards, candy and other gifts. These splurges can be fun, if adding to our debt, but they primarily benefit the High Priests of Commerce. Now Madison Avenue reigns over holidays. If that's not sick, I don't know what is.

A part of this empire involves moving family celebrations from home to the movie house. Here new cultural heroics and horrors are told in 3D with loud, wrap-around sound. Recent blockbuster movies like Clash of the Titans, Hannah Montana and Scary Movie 4 opened on Easter weekend. Other popular opening days are President's Day, Memorial Day, Halloween, Christmas, Thanksgiving Day and Independence Day. Whether these trends continue to grow or are replaced will be a matter of time, but the dates are all remnants of a time when millions of humans participated in the cycles observable on planet Earth.

If you interpret these observations about the ancients as promoting Paganism, I think you are missing the point. I am not promoting Paganism, Animalism, Witchcraft or Panentheism (the belief that God is in all material things). I am promoting integrity. We need more integrity with our earthland home if we hope to offer our children a healthy future.

The Empire And Us

Understanding today's empire is essential for today's entrepreneurs. If entrepreneurs are fashioned after the empire building mindset, their observations of the facts can suffer the same blindness. Common sense will not prevail. Integrity will not be achieved or maintained. Limited resources will not be equitably shared.

You and I are more a part of Nature than an empire. And when I think about all the Nature-endowed systems that work together and are necessary to walk, talk, imagine, adapt, reproduce, develop wisdom and skill, feel emotions, breathe, eliminate toxins and wastes, play, laugh and more... it seems a great miracle is being reduced to a material resource as important to an empire as a block of pavement.

In my conversations with others, I hear people say that they have faith in their efforts to build a better nation or a kingdom for God. But I ask about the evidence showing that this glut of building empires has sickened societies and the planet. Empires have not solved our most basic human problems including intense poverty, injustice, homelessness, chronic disease, war, hunger, classism, sexism and racism or political demagoguery. Can we really close our eyes to the disease symptoms of empire-building?

Institutional Judaism and Christianity may be making some strides toward becoming "green." Major corporations are also responding to public and scientific pressure to "go green." But a major change of perspective is required, not just a simple adjustment called "being green." We are at an ecological precipice and we need to remove the empire perspective from our minds. We are not here to build any kind of empire or serve any human master. We are here on this planet to support our family and community first, in harmony with the cycles and limits of the environment that gives us life. There is no other sustainable way.

Time for Nature's Return

Nature's cycles are about renewal and change. As Earth makes its revolutions around the sun, Nature's children can consciously be part of the revolution of their story. We do not need to be continually plagued by pollution, hunger and chronic disease. We can live long lives next to our families, but we will have to use a different story and stop feeding the voracious and corrupt system of consumer-powered empires.

If, like me, you are inclined to replace the old story of building a divinely sanctioned empire (it has had roughly three thousand years to prove itself), I can think of nothing better than spending time in Nature, learning from Nature and giving back. I am so renewed when I make time for my Nature walks. If you find reconnecting to Nature half as rewarding and fulfilling as I do, you will be well and satisfied instead of confused and driven to compete and complete the empire.

Nature's Nudge toward Community

Nature has given us a wonderful gift that is commonly referred to as the human community. As I mentioned earlier, most of us are not set up psychologically to be so self-reliant as to not need the companionship and assistance of other people. That level of self-sufficiency is a brutal existence.

So, our human ancestors gathered into tribes to survive the ebb and flow of Nature. In tribes, they looked out for one another, fed one another, protected and healed one another. Nature taught them to take care of one another like that. If they hadn't taken care of each other, everyone (especially the children) would have been more vulnerable to the elements, shelters would have been less protective, and clothing would never have developed into what we enjoy today. By living with others, we can diversify and add pleasures such as art, music, language, intellectual discourse, writing, organization, learning and more. This is one of Nature's best gifts to human beings.

For eons, communities have gathered around food- its production, storing and preparation. It can be a very satisfying occupation. It develops patience, observation, experimentation and community bonding and, as such, becomes the community's main investment. Until recently, most people on the earth made their living working the ground or tending to domesticated animals. Everyone had similar interests- weather, eating and perpetuating the cycle of life. I think it had a beautiful integrity. I am not saying it was easy or always productive. It wasn't. So humans sought new methods of food production including soil management, breeding, irrigation and, of course, supplication to the gods and goddesses of fertility.

Back then, humans tried to control Nature with prayer. "Sky, please send rain!" Or, "Stop raining, Clouds!" They prayed to elements of Nature or a deity to intervene. But with intelligent observation and experimentation, humans came to a better way of predicting outcomes and receiving a benefit. With this learning came predictability and opportunities for abundance. Nature was only asking for us to work directly with her.

Today's food barons (the RCMCs) know this better than anyone. On one front, they have dramatically increased corn production. According to the documentary "King Corn," a farmer in Iowa can now produce 200 bushels of grain on an acre that their grandparents could only get 40 bushels from. All over America, farmers are producing an excess of corn due to many advancements in irrigation, genetically modified seed, pesticides and chemical fertilizers.

Around the world, chemical fertilizers have boosted production. It is estimated that almost half of the world would not have food if chemical fertilizers weren't available.[28] This boost in food supply is largely responsible for the jump in population in the last one hundred years from 1.5 billion people to almost 7 billion, in spite of two world wars and over seventeen million more lives lost in major genocides during the same time.

The Resource Controlling Multinational Corporations have taken over major food markets besides corn production. Seeds. Fertilizers. Pesticides. Food processing. Food distribution. Fast food. Restaurant food. Meat production from beef and pork to poultry and fish. In most of these categories, four or five corporations own 30 to 80 percent of the market share.[29] They back their investments (maybe yours, too, if you play the stock market) with scientific study, political influence (PACs and lobbyists), effective advertising, marketing analysis and union busting, all the while simultaneously daily shipping billions of tons of products to their destinations.

The documentary "Food, Inc." puts the growth of the food conglomerates like this:

In the 1970s, the top five beef-packers controlled

---

[28] http://en.wikipedia.org/wiki/Chemical_fertilizer
[29] Food, Inc. documentary

only about 25% of the market. [Text: Top 5 beef packers: Armour, ibp, Swift, Morrell, ConAgra]

Today, the top four control more than 80% of the market. [Text: Cargill, Swift, Tyson, National Beef] You see the same thing happening now in pork. [Text: Smithfield, Swift, Cargill, Tyson]

Even if you don't eat at a fast food restaurant, you're now eating meat that's being produced by this system.

You look at the labels and you see Farmer this, Farmer that-- it's really just three or four companies that are controlling the meat.

We've never had food companies this big and this powerful in our history. Tyson, for example, is the biggest meat-packing company in the history of the world. The industry changed the entire way that chicken are raised.

Birds are now raised and slaughtered in half the time they were 50 years ago, but now they're twice as big. [Text: 1950: 70 days; 2008: 48 days] People like to

> *eat white meat, so they designed the chicken to have large breasts.*[30]

It all sounds impressive, but you may not know this: you often pay more than twice for your food. Your tax dollars went to the universities that studied growth yields so the RCMCs could put those discoveries into the fields. Your tax dollars fund much of the road system that ships the food to your town. Your tax dollars paid for government studies in agriculture and traffic efficiencies. Your tax dollars paid the farmer to plant his corn seed and to harvest it because the yield is so high that the market won't pay what it cost the farmer. Your tax dollars funded the law suit brought against the factory hog farm that is polluting the rivers and taxes went to clean up the toxins in the rivers.

Your ancestors' tax dollars were spent to support them in the Supreme Court when the RCMCs argued that they have just as much right as you do to keep their records private (and therefore, unanswerable to the citizens or the government). Unfortunately, you lost that case along with

---

[30] Food, Inc, Documentary by Robert Kenner, starring food experts Michael Pollan and Eric Schlosser

your ancestors and the RCMCs won[31].

What's after dinner?

I want you to hear this point of discussion; it's important. If the RCMCs are willing to do this to our food, what else are they willing to do?

This is just to put food on our table. What about getting our other basic needs met? What are they doing to force us to pay their expenses *there*? Such as: our investments for retirement or college? Our home? Our need for factual information? The responsiveness of our elected representatives? The safety of our identity? Our income? Our dependence on oil? They are involved in every one of those of sectors. And they have established rights there. Should we trust them to keep this economy going forward? Will their "going green" be beneficial to us or will it primarily benefit them?

The food delivery system is considered a success for the RCMC's. And they have their eyes on capturing each and every other resource delivery system that we have come to depend upon. RCMC's already control the delivery of news

---

[31] Timeline of Personhood
http://reclaimdemocracy.org/personhood/personhood_timeline.pdf

and information, the transportation industry, fashion and cosmetics, home appliances, energy, the money and credit we require for exchange, and they are making inroads into controlling the delivery of water. As a notable example, Monsanto has taken an aggressive approach to own every plantable crop by patenting the seed genomes. Human genes are being patented as I write this and the pharmaceutical industry is cataloging to own every plant derivative in the disappearing rain forests. I swear, if the RCMC's could find a way to charge us for the air we breathe, they would.

This approach to the gifts of Nature is one of capture and control for profit rather than an approach of sharing and respect. I believe that the resources we need for life and trade are community property. They belong to each one of us. The resources of our small planet are not the property of a small group of investors!

The day, water, sun, moon, night- I do not have to purchase these things with money. -Titus Maccius Plautus

Nature, our way back

Nature is the one thing that connects us all. It is calling us back. The very essence of Nature is in each one of us. We don't need any corporation to lead the way to Nature. (I don't mean to imply that we should let them off the hook. They need to clean up their act and clean up their waste, just like we must.)

Nature even endowed us with a return vehicle and hid it in our very selves. We have no excuses for not knowing the way back, it is through the local community, doing things with and for Nature and each other. It is that simple. The Native Americans exemplified this with their round homes, arranged in a circle around the fire. This way, they watched for each other, knew their neighbor and their neighbor's family. They hunted, cooked and repaired as community projects. They observed Nature and told her stories.

But didn't they lose the war for the land, you ask? Listen to the wise words of Chief Seattle. He nailed it.

> *But why should I mourn at the untimely fate of my people? Tribe follows tribe, and nation follows nation, like the waves of the sea. It is the order of nature, and regret is useless. Your time of decay may be*

distant, but it will surely come, for even the White Man whose God walked and talked with him as friend to friend, cannot be exempt from the common destiny. We may be brothers after all. We will see.

The way back to Nature is community by community. And, as the community that Nature pulled together here and now, we must lead the way back to Nature. Or, section six will be invoked: divided we will fall.

Section Five Summary: Nature is what holds us all together. From sun up to sun up, we are products of Nature. We live on a small planet that is home to all of us and it is shared with millions of other species. For a few thousand years now, humans have been losing touch with Nature. Building empires for men and gods has driven us to developments we call "civilized" but are out of touch with Nature, each other and our own physical makeup. The resulting empires have sponsored national jealousies, religious and ethnic purges and a million other inhumanities. Despite the acknowledgment of the planet's fragility, we need more than slogans written on 20% recycled paper. We need businesses and communities in integrity with Nature. Now is the time for Earth's children to renew the hope of our children, while there is time to salvage some of it.

If you tell a lie big enough and keep repeating it, people will eventually come to believe it. – Joseph Goebbels, Reich Minister of Propaganda

Chapter Six, Divided We Fall

Have you ever witnessed neighbors "crossing swords" over competing team loyalties?

Were you there when the insult was about someone's car choice?

If not, you certainly have heard disrespect for someone that voted "wrong."

These are not signs of confidence or freedom; they are indicators of being dominated.

To Divide is to Conquer

You may have heard the analogy about how easy it is to break five or six single sticks compared to a bundle of the same sticks. This analogy is often used for the strengths of being a team or many being of one mind. (China's unity is a living example- their unity as a people of one race and their refusal to being divided into fiefdoms has helped them resist would-be conquerors for several centuries.) Dividing a people is perhaps the most effective weapon against them. Division among an enemy's ranks will compromise them without lifting a sword. This principle was ensconced in military literature when Sun Tzu wrote about it in The Art of War.

Creating divisions works as effectively on the home front as it does on the battlefield. In peacetime, an oppressive, or simply opportunistic, regime uses division to prevent a collective mind among the populace. Division keeps the majority of lower and middle income families from leaving their place.

The issue for entrepreneurs is not about war tactics, but how the RCMCs use their influence and power, especially within the media and the economy, to keep us divided and off balance. You may be aware of some of these tactics, or not. In either case, please do not skip over the tactics touched on in this section. It is tactically significant for us to understand the culture creators.

The power of "one up"

Chief among dividing strategies is the hierarchical system. In it, those on the top of the pyramid have the most power and resources to maintain power; on the bottom are those with the least power and minimal resources.

Everyone is involved... and by assuming their place, each person validates and perpetuates it. Employers and managers, teachers and governmental bodies, money and institutional religions create systems in which some people get more power, influence or consideration than others.

Even when the hierarchy does not involve things of value (such as money, houses and bonuses), the arrangement has the same effect as dividing limited resources unequally. Those at the top get the fatty, succulent cream (such as powerful connections, respect and best opportunities), and those at the bottom get the watery non-fat version.

Fellow citizens, this is not what the Founding Fathers had

in mind when they started this country. More than anything, this country became a strong nation by virtue of a large middle class. It was shaped more like a watermelon than a pyramid. And my bet is that struggling to get to the top isn't what you look forward to when you get up every morning.

Unless you are a living saint, owning less than someone else *always* creates envy or dissatisfaction. We have all experienced it. This feeling of receiving or being less than someone else urges us toward acquisition for ourselves and reducing what others have. Hierarchy creates divisions by establishing resource scarcity.

Every day the news tells stories of people that have more money, power, influence and consideration than we do...unless we happen to be Oprah Winfrey or Bill Gates.

Our feelings of inferiority are stirred every day with a potent blast of at least 3000 commercial or branding messages.

Our inferior position is enforced when religious worship requires its members to kneel (physically or in spirit) to an all powerful judge and to blindly obey the deity's ministers.

Every blockbuster movie or TV show, and many of the foods we eat, remind us, if we are half conscious, that we are all slaves to urges and brand loyalties.

This feeling of inferiority makes us feel starved for more life, more respect, and more tokens of authority. We behave like children in a sibling rivalry and less like responsible adults capable of making room for others as we make our own way.

When we don't get enough, we work the system for more, whether or not it deprives others of the same. We create divisions that justify to ourselves why "they" don't deserve what we do. We become guarded, retreat into our home base (where our belongings and systems define us), and our generosity is held in check. The last thing we think of is to challenge the reality that sets us up.

How did it get this way?

The attack on our unity as human communities is pervasive.

- False and misleading advertising.
- False history/ omission of events and facts.
- Propaganda/ Disinformation.
- Media distractions and distortions.
- The RCMCs' merciless profit motive.
- Imaginary divisions such as sports team loyalties, politics, religion, brand snobbery.

- Schools that fail to teach us critical thinking, financial and common sense.
- Overly competitive work environments that foster stress and reactive thinking.
- Longer work hours and creeping money pressures.
- A complex and antagonistic legal system.

All this has been engineered to divide us.

Programmed Disempowerment

William Randolph Hearst was the first king of media. His empire took hold of multiple media channels (newspapers, books, magazines, news services and movies) from the late 1800's until the 1930's. Using yellow journalism, cheaper rates, financial backing and influence, Hearst manufactured the popular vote from New York to Los Angeles. Ultimately, he controlled 38 newspapers across the country, 28 of which were major publications.

The story behind the curtain is that Hearst was the first media magnate to take the assignment of broadcasting propaganda for the US government and monopolistic corporations. It started with newspaper stories about the war effort which spread to other venues including film. In one particular effort, Hearst inundated the public with tales of horror over cannabis, since the manufacture of cheaper hemp-based paper threatened his massive paper-mill holdings.[32] His sensational stories and inaccurate arguments stirred up fears about Mexican laborers that still linger almost a century later. Little did the public realize how their strings were being pulled.

The media does more than intentionally spread misinformation. 1984 by George Orwell depicts other manipulative techniques made possible by programmed information to keep the people passive. One tactic is giving confusing information. Although this tactic is anti-intuitive, it works effectively in propaganda, hypnosis and brainwashing. When faced with confusing information, subjects question their critical thinking and wander into beliefs that are not in their best interests. Media use this "freedom of the press" to fan the flames of controversy. It not only sells newspapers, and of course, advertising, controversy keeps people at odds with each other.

In cultures not tied by modern media, they spend more time (a lot more time) outdoors. After (or during) their day labors, they are likely to walk to and through the marketplace. There they linger over the smells, colors and

---

[32] http://en.wikipedia.org/wiki/Legal_history_of_cannabis_in_the_United_States

textures of vegetables, fruits, breads and meats. They seem keen on having real, fresh food. Rather than driving from store to store to get the advertised specials at Ralph's and Von's supermarkets, life is a day by day working celebration of seasons and cycles. Fresh spices may be purchased, plucked from the roadside or picked from the garden. The meal is created amidst family talk; connecting is layered with shared sensual input. The TV is not on during meal time. (This is how most of the world operates.) They are more dependent on local news provided by people they know (and that they expect to know their whole life).

The average American, by contrast, spends over six hours a day being entertained, soothed or put to sleep (literally and figuratively) by television. Media abounds with radio, newspapers and magazines, movies, and signs of every sort. And then, let's not forget the nearly 200 million internet users in the US that spend an average of thirteen hours a week online.[33]

It must be obvious to any objective observer that people that are presented several hours a day with potent images, emotional storylines and quirky humor would think differently from those that are not so engaged. There is no

---

[33] http://news.cnet.com/8301-1023_3-10421016-93.html

way to avoid the impact. And it doesn't do any good to convince yourself that you aren't really watching TV, that it is just background noise to keep you company. By the way, have you noticed just one fifth (a thousand per day) of the five thousand commercial messages that confront you daily?[34] No. You haven't seen that many. This is an ideal state for culture creators to impact our minds- when our critical faculties are on vacation. And don't think that they don't know it!

But I only watch public television!

I have heard all sorts of arguments for watching television, including a reliance on news and sports only or a preference for public television or other "educational" programs. (Have you ever wondered why TV shows are called "programming?") But the evidence says that the medium cannot be salvaged for people with integrity. I am not the only one with that opinion.

Consider former, successful ad executive Jerry Mander, owner of a major advertising firm. He became so good at manipulating people's choices that he began to have second thoughts. He switched his efforts to educational

---

[34] http://www.nytimes.com/2007/01/15/business/media/15everywhere.html

television hoping to use his skills only for "good"... but he saw the same dynamics there. His book, <u>Four Arguments for the Elimination of Television</u> is a tour de force exposé that has not been equaled since its publication in 1978.

I read with fascination the February 23, 2002 article published by Scientific American establishing that television mimics the horizontal view that is similar to the first upright primates. Mixed with movement, it triggers an almost irrepressible biological response associated with food or a significant threat.[35]

I challenge people to give up their TV. It is impossible to have your own mind when others are telling you what to think, what to value and who you are. But TV has a pull like no other medium. Going unplugged is perhaps harder than going on a diet. With all the twelve step programs available, it is funny no one ever goes to TV Addicts Anonymous.

I spy with my little eye

Television trains us to pursue personal pleasure first, not community advancement. It convinces us that we deserve it, every bit as much as those "people" inside the box

---

[35] Scientific American Feb. 23, 2002 "Television Addiction Is No Mere Metaphor" by Robert Kubey and Mihaly Csikszentmihalyi

deserve it. We are cajoled to ask for more and to get it for less money, and we come to "know" that *things* are what make us feel good about ourselves.

Television is effective at making men feel like crap if we aren't six foot five with the look of a quarterback. It gives women age-modified studio models for comparison. Compared to them, we easily conclude that our ass is too big, our thighs and bellies are embarrassing, we have sagging breasts and facial skin. New bright and spicy models appear every episode, looking us in the eye as we age and bulge.

Is it any wonder that we are a nation addicted to anti-depressants more than all other countries combined? Do we not see that these select models are professionally made up, airbrushed, under perfect lighting and photo-altered in a controlled studio to appear eternally youthful? Do we really believe the cars they drive and the smiles they flash are who we are or should be?

And the beauty of it all for the drivers of the consumerist culture is that even though we know the TV people are not real, the effect is the same: we believe. We believe the artificial reality carefully engineered by those that benefit most. The producers know we believe because we buy, even to our peril.

Engineered Cycles

Have you ever noticed that about every twelve or so years, we "need" another war? That about every eight to ten years, we dip into another recession that closes down small and medium-sized businesses? That about every eight to twelve years, we see a shift in political tide, from Republican to Democrat predominance but the people and policies pretty much stay the same? Lately, these cycles seem to be shortening, but they still swing back and forth. These are not natural like the tides. These shifts are essential to the engineered marketplace.

These up and down shifts are how the capitalists buy low and sell high. The cycles are how in a failing market (announced in the headlines), assets are moved from one sector to another. (For example, money from major pension plans move into the accounts of brokers or from old factory towns to investors' pockets.) It's how middle class and small business ventures are guaranteed to flounder.

Recognizing the inevitability and regularity of these cycles helps the Entrepreneur That Could avoid the worst. Gone are the days that a family business can be built and inherited. It is no longer financially feasible to build a small business into a large one. By virtue of their destructive nature and frequency, these cycles are effective at keeping arising powers from competing with established players.

This doesn't mean that small businesses are a lost cause; it means small business must observe the situation and adapt accordingly. It means financial strategies must be more diversified, flexible and business savvy. In light of the cycles, I would also argue that the better investments are in the community, education and food self-sufficiency. Never invest in Wall Street, unless, like George Soros and Warren Buffett, you KNOW the folks creating the business cycles.

Easy money on Wall Street

To open a casino, you start with investors. These business people know that both investors and players like "easy money." The rules are set to ensure that "the house" and its investors win most of the time all the while attracting gamblers for a chance at some "easy money." Growth happens by attracting more investors and players through a polished image of the opportunity and the introduction of new games that "earn" easy money. (Are we talking here about casinos or Wall Street here? It seems these principles belong to both.)

Players are lured to casinos by promises of winning, brilliant lights, exciting bells, intoxicating drinks and girls wearing next to nothing. Less perceptible, many gambling areas have extra oxygen pumped in and use interior lights that mimic sunrise. It is full sensual immersion. When the players lose, they go home and tell everyone that they had a great time. (Having a good time justifies the losses.) The money they lost is enough to pay the investors, employees and for adding more brilliant lights, exciting bells, intoxicating drinks and girls wearing next to nothing. This attracts more people willing to take a chance at winning easy money.

Both Wall Street and casinos do the simple repetition of attracting capital, then subtracting from that capital. Attract-Subtract. Attract-Subtract. The money that investors lose on Wall Street doesn't disappear as we tend to think. Neither do losses at the gambling halls just disappear. The losses become another investor's gain or it belongs to "the house."

Where does the money go that was "lost" on Wall Street? While it goes many places, you can bet that the trading houses and their traders take the majority of it. The wealth "invested" in Wall Street for the last twenty, thirty and forty years, from airline pilots to factory line workers, has been reduced 70%. In spite of the enticing names Wall Street gives these funds (Traditional and Roth IRA's, tax deferred 401K's and Employee Stock options), the gains on those losses did not go to the pension funds, corporate accounts and banks that put their assets on the block.... the money now belongs to the house. The average stock broker's salary is at least twice the average national wage earner's and currently attracts our universities' brightest students.

Who can we blame? No one but ourselves. Did we not know that the game was rigged to the house's advantage? Now, the game of real estate is being exposed for the gamble it really is.

October. This is one of the peculiarly dangerous months to speculate in stocks in. The others are July, January, September, April, November, May, March, June, December, August and February.
- Mark Twain

The Corporate Age, When the Founding Fathers Lost

Businesses sold on Wall Street are a completely different animal from businesses that primarily serve a Main Street need. Once these local businesses "go public" they achieve most of their profit from being traded on the stock exchange. No longer are they primarily motivated by real market needs with products and services. (This is not to say that they don't provide products and services, only that those products and services become secondary.)

How did it get this way? It started around the end of the Civil War, when corporations' activities and political involvement were specifically restricted in their charter. The charter (fashioned after the specific rights to buy and sell granted by a sovereign monarch) was an agreement between the corporation and the local community.

1865. The Civil War was over. The South surrendered begrudgingly with heavy losses. This battle cost the eleven southern states 30% of their able men between 20 and 45. Their workforce of an estimated four million slaves were freed by the President's emancipation acts and the 13th Amendment, making slavery illegal. During Reconstruction, which lasted for another twelve years, bitterness, corruption and rivalries divided families, parishes, counties and states.

The Federal Government expanded its authority during Reconstruction to put displaced slaves onto land, establish new civic authorities and reestablish trade. Congress wrangled authority from President Lincoln's successor in this time of political turmoil. Fields and railroads lay decimated. Women had to work harder to replace their deceased men, disabled men and slaves. Within all the misery (I don't believe it got much public attention) corporations grew by leaps and bounds.

The 14th amendment (ratified in 1868, it gave freed slaves the right of due process of law before their property could be confiscated) was taken by corporations as a legal precedent to hold property privately and to operate autonomously from the interests of the community. (I know this sounds ridiculous; read the record if you don't believe me.) Reconstruction also allowed corporations to grow financially as they scored contracts to rebuild and construct new railroads. They learned to use the political system like a favorite playground, leased federal land for cheap, determined which towns would survive and which ones would collapse and generally filled in where the government was weak. They were the forerunners of today's Resource Controlling Multinational Corporations.

The expansion of the Federal Government and government-sanctioned corporations during this time of confusion and loss firmly buried community controls.

Corporations became co-creators of the economic environment, whether it was a city or rural. In case after court case, large, well-funded corporations won rights to grow and operate outside of real community needs. Thusly, communities became helpless to determine their own economic destiny. While this cannot be called slavery or a totalitarian form of governance, it is a form of hierarchy left unchecked by the public interest.

The Market Fallacy

Mega-sized corporations benefiting from this change of events say that they respond to "the market." This ignores the fact that "the market" is created by "the house," has no actual voice and no conscience. It does not have self-regulating integrity. It does not offer social value, nor does it uphold the values that keep a community viable. "The market" is not necessarily the public interest.

The market does not think about the full range of costs of business operations, such as the highways, the schools, the environment, the social supports (such as child care) on which it depends. Public activism and outcry was required for unethical, monopolistic corporations to become responsible for the costs of worker safety, worker health, training and vacation. Clearly, the corporation's interests were not in human health and safety.

We could interpret these events as indicators of poor corporate management... or it could be another example of the ways that the profit motive (or the "free market" as the RCMCs define it) divides workers against their employers, their government, the environment, schools and even family members.

Beliefs divide us

This is no shocker. Beliefs have divided people for as long as societies have been formed. Look at caste systems and classes. Religions and politics. Races and languages. Self-protective beliefs make people prone to believe that others are less than they are. This is a far cry from the kind of tolerance and brilliance of spirit that made the United States of America a reality and, later, a great economic power. It is our tolerance that helps people overcome differences, real or imagined, and achieve something otherwise unattainable.

I believe that the Founding Fathers would be proud of creating the first country to make religious tolerance a founding principle. But why do modern Americans allow other beliefs to divide us? Why do we fight over sports teams or a neighborhood address? Why do we defer to people that went to "better" schools? Why does a person's homemade wardrobe make a difference to us if that person is a conscientious contributor to our community, their family or military? Why do we prefer to see the differences that potentially divide us rather than the differences that make us strong and interconnected?

Today's Americans don't operate like a community of supportive farmers or back in the days of self-reliant tradespeople. They were connected to each other in a united effort to keep government and monopolies like the East India Trading Company out of their affairs. Those that had land fought to make sure it stayed unclaimed by the government. They loved their freedom from government control more than depending on rules that came from "on high."

We're divided, often against each other, and it is exacerbated by design of the Resource Controlling Multinational Corporations.

Hierarchy in the Work Place

We all feel the stress of competing for our jobs these days. If our employers don't remind us that someone else would feel lucky to have our job, the news media reminds us that more jobs were just shipped out to Asia or south of the border. Ruthless cutbacks of loyal company personnel are hardly news anymore. If we get a new job, we might notice that the new employment contracts allow our bosses to fire us without notice and without reason. Our bosses constantly require us to do work that is not in our job description, stay late and fill in for staff that has been fired. As if meeting our sales goals wasn't stressful enough!

Competition for raises within a business can also be fierce. A funny example is found among winners of state lotteries and heirs of large estates. It has been reported that if these folks stay on the job, other workers expect them to step aside so those with less money have improved chances to get promoted. They are regularly turned down for advancement if it is known that they have become well off. So, the rush of money pits co-workers against them, even if they are conscientious and able workers.

Competing for limited jobs and pay is a way large corporations limit their liabilities to the human equation. They ask us to take more of the risk of doing business. And we must take those increased risks at a time when the loss of our job can literally put our family on the streets. Yes, employee morale is low, job loyalty is low and some statistician is stating that the recession is about "the market." Ridiculous!

Legal Overload

I am appalled at what has happened over the last 40 years. We are overloaded with regulations and red tape for the simplest things. Common sense has gone out the window! Gone are the days when the law operated on the basis of common law, the assumption that we are all adults with a common aim, that there are many ways to accomplish good things and that we are innocent until proven guilty. Laws pile on top of laws to expressly forbid certain ways of doing things that could possibly lead to harm, a legal entanglement or fraud. The result is more legal entanglements, more litigation, more enemies and more stalled government. Legal overload effectively pits us against one another for the sole purpose of taking our focus off of the ways that RCMCs ride roughshod over community (read: common) values.

Overuse of legal language is another pet peeve. Look at the kind of contracts required now to buy a house, a car or to take out a simple loan. And what about the long forms of

End User License Agreements attached to each piece of computer software? The way EULAs read to me is that they take my money and then have the legal right to not provide support or instructions all the while denying any guarantee that it will work! And I click "I Agree." Every time.

The language in these common everyday contracts bullies us into compliance. The obtuse legalese is not something we have any time or expertise to understand. They are designed to make us feel stupid, confused and submissive. And it doesn't have to be this way!

Alan Siegel is a former IBM executive who has made it his mission to simplify our overly complex and incomprehensible contracts. One of his projects was to reword the typical credit application of six pages into one easy page. It is complete and completely legal without the extended legal jargon. He has also been hired to revise tax forms and employee contracts that are typically more about impressive hierarchical gobbledygook than information.

I am advising my contacts to put their foot down on this divisive tactic: refuse to sign any agreement that is not in plain English. If you can't understand it, don't sign it. Tell your lender that legalese is offensive. Understand that complex clauses wrapped around threats of legal action do not build a nation. Insist on your freedom, common sense and plain English.

And for common sense sake, don't ask your employees or contractors to agree to obtuse legalese in your agreements.

Getting back to our own design

Real human satisfaction comes from unity with others, meaningful struggle and sharing. Instead, we play assigned roles in a consumerist driven economy. We value competition and acquisition more than cooperation and complementation. We live in a struggle for market position and access to power that can never satisfy us. With increased separation comes more fear, cynicism and lack of trust. At some point, we lose control of these emotions and business gives way to protecting a false reality.

The RCMC vision and design is not for gathered communities of integrated support. Think about it. This is no longer the America that put farmers on a pedestal, respected for their hard work to grow all the food we need. Back in the day, it was like this: "Yeah, Farmer Roberts has the finest corn you will ever eat. If you have that on your table you are extremely lucky." "The McGrew farms have the best turkeys for hundreds of miles, I believe. Those turkeys are truly worth waiting for. We got one last year and used it for about a dozen meals."

We don't hear people valuing their neighbors or earnestly supporting community based businesses. We typically don't stand up for community members or for their right to have a different opinion. We don't gather at the market or talk over the common fence. Local business owners are treated like transients unless they can compete on price and delivery. Our current state is more important to us than the possibilities for understanding and shared community goals.

I am not saying this to scold you, my neighbor. I am asking all of us for an honest reevaluation- because there is a way out. But first, we have to admit to a problem. Then we have to believe that we are powerful enough to change it...or someone already itching to govern our lives (and common resources) will decide for us.

Self or RCMC Definition?

We all operate from our self definition. But ever since our environment (work, familial, food, residential and governance) has been engineered by corporations, we have operated according to a definition given to us by others. We are literally dependent on corporations we don't know (with policies we don't understand) for our food, money, jobs, protection from harm. education and recreation. We call ourselves lovers of freedom, but we stay in our place. We call ourselves responsible adults but couldn't feed ourselves for a week if the supermarkets closed.

Our basic personal and communal needs are not complicated.

They are:

- Our people (tribe/ community),
- Food and water,
- Industry (getting things done),
- Shelter and land,
- Recreation,
- A level of security (fear abatement),
- Trade,
- Meaning and language,
- Growth, and
- A self-understanding within a tribal story.

These elements allow us to be human and content as members of an ecosystem. We are told that the American

Indians had all of this without a form of official government. They prospered into developed civilizations without a written language but with poetry and songs, a tribal history and a complex way of cooperating with the environment.

In this rich land with abundant space and resources, every one of those human needs has been re-engineered by the powerful Resource Controlling Multinational Corporations.

- Our tribe is largely designed by the economic forces we had no say in creating. Often our tribe has been broken up due to the demands of "the marketplace." Our tribes are no longer family and working towns, but friends we collect and depart with as our jobs call us away.

- Our food (and sometimes our water) comes to us through a large and complex food industry. We don't comprehend what the packaged meat is made of or how our frozen foods get processed. We might as well be driving a car as eating a meal. Put in the key and go.

- Industry has been specialized and systematized. We leave our homes, not to go to the orchard or field to get our necessary implements and food. We must do something else first that meets the needs of an employer, a government body or a client.

- Shelter and land is not just putting up a home for our growing family. It is a highly regulated and speculative industry driven and manipulated by Wall Street.

- Recreation is largely defined by our modern high-tech toys: TV, iPods and MP3 players, DVD players, gameboy-type interactive games, computers and internet, movie theaters... Rarely does a family or tribe gather for games that connect them, teach them and bind them with fun and food. Someone other than the tribal elders are creating our interactions through re-engineered recreation. Facebook and Twitter interactions, the new social hubs, are characterized by discussions and announcements about celebrities, movies, music, politics and news, all media created by the culture-makers.

- A level of security is necessary, and due to many factors, we hire keepers of the law instead of doing our own neighborhood security. The Native Americans did not require police forces or jails to deal with their less than ideal citizens. Because we have more jailed citizens than any other industrialized nation, it is time to reevaluate the effectiveness of this product of the industrial system.

- Trade is a good thing, bringing in products a local economy cannot support. Business has never been more controlled and regulated by government and large corporations. This has been good for large businesses and very bad for small business. It also taxes small businesses to the breaking point. And many good local businesses cannot compete with the RCMCs' monopolies.

- Meaning and language are necessary for trade and security. Yet much of our meaning has been created by advertisers that tell us we are not good enough as we are, by government restrictions that threaten steep fines and jail, by the entertainment industry of celebrities that flash and crash, and by institutional religions that promote guilt and submission. What healthy meaning can come from that?

- Growth is normally a part of evolution and discovery. But not all growth is good. (See "cancer.") 1. Our population continues to grow beyond healthy limits.

2. Our educational growth is stifled. 3. Our war technology still develops, killing more with ever-increasing precision. 4. Our national and personal debt is ballooning. 5. Our technology growth is impressive due to heavy RCMC investment. That is one good out of five growth types, all to the credit of the RCMCs.

- Self understanding comes within a tribal story. Here the RCMCs have really nailed us. Our self-understanding and story is like hand and glove with the economy, an economy established according to the dictates of the rich and powerful. Middle and poor classes are officially relegated to the trickle down effect with the RCMCs holding the ladle. If that wasn't bad enough, Wall Street's growth holds us captive. It is that simple. All our training and efforts come to nothing if Wall Street collapses. It is the rat race we never got to bet on.

God help us.

Not unlike the formula for Twelve Step programs, our addiction to consumer spending, financial insolvency and unsound business must be acknowledged. To regain our integrity, our failures must be named. We could start with these:

> We have become susceptible to a hierarchical structure that divides up the benefits of life on this planet unequally.
>
> We came to believe the proclamations of self-interested institutions.
>
> We doubted our ability to approach God in our own right or that God was present within us.
>
> We accepted the judgment of paid-off experts and professionals in determining what is best for us and our bodies.
>
> We listened to politicians that told us that they can best solve our problems with legislation, incentives and studies.
>
> We believed that we will be better if we get the latest model car or technology.
>
> We give deference to elected leaders that spoke about equality but made back room deals with their cronies and cheated on their spouses.
>
> We allowed Wall Street and the banks to sell us down the river of loss and debt.
>
> We buried our heads in the sand, delighted with the

prospect that all the conveniences, abundance, style, food and energy we need would be taken care of.

We trusted our God-given passions to inspire and drive our business calculations.

After acknowledging our deal with the devil, it is time to believe that we can, with persistence, tolerance, integrity and common sense, solve every problem we put our minds to understand.

We don't need a hierarchical structure to achieve what we value most.

We believe in the human process of community unbound by profit motivations.

We trust in the God presence entrusted to each and every one of us.

We value our intuition and community feedback for personal decision making.

We take exception to professional politicians that do not live and thrive next to us.

We find our identity in our contributions of wealth and wisdom to the community and tribe rather than personal ownership of possessions.

We do not live beyond our means because to do so indebts all of our connections.

We budget and respect our resources, replenishing and restoring the requirements of the children for coming generations.

We build our businesses on proven markets with established skills and to serve real community needs.

Let's own up to our bad choices and be done with it. We can see what it has come to. Let's unplug, connect to people and learn how powerful we are. Let's listen to those that have gone before us without corporate control. Let's be intelligent about putting to use the business brilliance that is committed to solving every major human problem including cancer, heart disease, homelessness, cheap energy, illiteracy and every prejudice.

Section Seven will give us tools to move forward:

- Ways to make a contribution, but not in competition with, or the manner of, the RCMCs;
- A Founding Father's way of understanding cash;
- Taking responsibility for our food sources;

- Understanding risk and reducing it within the community.

Section Six Summary: Divided people are not strong for each other or for protecting themselves. The RCMCs have used several methods of division including hierarchy, engineered cycles, mass media, education, institutionalized religion, property and brand loyalties. Propaganda, profits, overwork and over-regulation drive us farther from our communal strength.

Corporate greed got its grip on government after the Civil War. Government-sanctioned corporations justified their iron fist as "market pressures" and pitted workers against one another. Surely every basic human need became re-engineered: community, food, industry, shelter, recreation, security, trade, meaning, growth and self-understanding. We have grown dependent on the false economy and no longer experience our source of strength: our connection to community and nature. We must admit our addiction and use our collective minds to solve real needs.

If there is no struggle there is no progress. Those who profess to favor freedom and yet deprecate agitation...want crops without plowing up the ground, they want rain without thunder and lightning. They want the ocean without the awful roar of its many waters... Power concedes nothing without a demand. It never did and it never will. – Frederick Douglass

Section 7, Stopping the Insanity/ Inviting the Entrepreneur's Revolution

I am reminded of dreamers that came before you and me, men and women with a vision of justice, freedom of conscience, collective participation and shared responsibility. (The Founding Fathers come to mind.) It shows that my vision is no more outlandish. In fact, "The Entrepreneur That Could" has been done before- just not with the technology and communication that is available to us now. We can profit and succeed in ways that make sense and are beneficial to our source of life, the planet's marvelously complex, yet balanced ecosystem.

As these dreamers told of their vision, through speeches, banners, pamphlets and demonstrations, listeners experienced a spark of recognition. The glow of that spark ignited a fever of light. What we need now is my spark and your spark, a shared ignition that fuels emerging business strategies of community shared integrity.

In 1876, one hundred years after the Declaration of Independence, many American citizens felt compelled by the circumstances to issue new forms of Declarations of Independence. One party, The Workingmen's Party of Illinois, expressed their disgust of corporate greed and abuses with the following flaming indictment. It stirred a fever of light not unknown to lovers of freedom as it declared their rational need for self-reliance.

"The present system has enabled capitalists to make laws in their own interests to the injury and oppression of the workers.

It has made the name Democracy, for which our forefathers fought and died, a mockery and a shadow, by giving to property an unproportionate amount of representation and control over Legislation.

It has enabled capitalists. . . to secure government aid, inland grants and money loans, to selfish railroad corporations, who, by monopolizing the means of transportation are enabled to swindle both the producer and the consumer.

It has allowed the capitalists, as a class, to appropriate annually 5/6 of the entire production of the country....

It has therefore prevented mankind from fulfilling their natural destinies on earth—crushed out ambition, prevented marriages or caused false and unnatural ones—has shortened human life, destroyed morals and fostered crime, corrupted judges, ministers, and statesmen, shattered confidence, love and honor among men, and made life a selfish, merciless struggle for existence instead of a noble and generous struggle for perfection, in which equal advantages should be given to all, and human lives relieved from an unnatural and degrading competition for bread.

We, therefore, the representatives of the workers of Chicago, in mass meeting assembled, do solemnly publish and declare ...That we are absolved from all allegiance to the existing political parties of this country, and that as free and independent producers we shall endeavor to acquire the full power to make our own laws, manage our own production, and govern ourselves, acknowledging no rights without duties, no duties without rights. And for the support of this declaration, with a firm reliance on the assistance and cooperation of all workingmen, we mutually pledge to each other our lives, our means, and our sacred honor."

The men who signed that declaration went on to fight and die for the above principles. They were eventually divided and crushed. Today, our loyalties still do not belong to the rich and powerful. It does not belong to the government that allows corporations to take away our jobs and the industries that made us economically strong. It does not belong to sports teams, designer labels or Ivy League schools.

Common sense loyalty does belong to a vital economy that functions in the best interests of its workers, small business owners, as well as dependents and retirees. I believe that the cure for our economy, our social stability, our health and nutrition, government, jobs and education is for us to become a nation of vital entrepreneurs- entrepreneurs taking action in a positive paradigm that supports who we truly are. Who are we? It comes down to this. We are brilliant innovators with a love for our community and its future.

The economy does not belong to a few that seem to command the most money and assets. The national economy belongs to *all who are dependent upon it for their livelihood.* (The exception is the entities outside our national boundaries. Our economy does not belong to them. Nor does it belong to those inside that believe they can manipulate our economy from the outside.)

It is time for the government to support the ideal of entrepreneurial effort they say makes America great, not the greed driven top 10% of the population that control 85% of the assets.[36] If the government does not listen, the American people are not obligated to adhere to their inequitable policies, laws and regulations.

---

[36] http://sociology.ucsc.edu/whorulesamerica/power/wealth.html. According to this article, the top 1% of Americans own 34.6% of the country's privately held wealth and the next 19% own 50.5%, meaning that the top 20% own 85%. This leaves the bottom 80% with 15%. In terms of financial wealth alone (not residence), the top 1% own 42.7% of privately held wealth.

Let's look again at the document that established the rights and responsibilities of the American people and their government, The Declaration of Independence.

"[A]ll men are created equal [and] endowed by their Creator with certain unalienable rights... to secure these rights, Governments are instituted...whenever any Government becomes destructive of these ends [life, liberty and the pursuit of happiness], it is the Right of the People to alter or to abolish it and to institute a new Government.[37]"

Allow me to point out two factors that the Founding Fathers hammered out with precision.

1. The government's job is to secure and protect our unalienable rights- not control freedoms, limit access, protect big business or restrict information!

2. The nation's people, as the governed, have a God-given right to alter or abolish and institute their governments. No government has the right to oppose the will of the governed.

These bold statements of defiance in the Declaration of Independence and the declaration of 1876 from the labor forces of Chicago were written after many attempts to procure peace and honor for all concerned. The list of

---

[37] The Declaration of Independence is found in Supplement Two, p. 244

offenses in both declarations was long and recorded for history. The workers and colonists had finally reached their limit. In declaring independence, they proclaimed all previously established laws null and void. Then the colonists forced the lackeys back to where they came from. That is the legacy they left for us to re-establish.

The future begins at school.

Schools are where our impressionable children learn about who they are in community. If we want a better future, let's teach them in school about personal finance, personal responsibility, geography and care of our earth home, how our political system works (or doesn't), and to always ask questions. Education shouldn't be about making kids similarly book smart. It should be about self-reliance, local ecology, diplomacy and conflict resolution, common sense, community and family relationships, educating themselves through all of life, reading great literature that inspires independent thinking and action, discovering their gifts, nutrition, how to study and command a subject. These are more important than IQ testing, sports and competing for grades.

Let's let them show their brilliance even if it doesn't fit a factory role or an assembly line paper trail. Let's believe that they can lead us into the future with new insights into transportation, communication, health, restoring the environment, creating peace among differences....Let's let them win without making others lose, choosing goals based on participation and personal improvement. Let's give the children with special needs the support only a community can give- personal attention, encouragement to be who they are and offer them technological solutions that remove their major obstacles.

Let's teach them about nutrition so their bodies will not be challenged by junk food, so they can learn self-sufficiency, so they taste, feel and smell the glorious fruits direct from the earth. Let us lead them through acts of service and humility so they might serve their future generations with compassion and without greed. Let us place their needs before our own, their future ahead of ours.

The earning timeline

The reason we do this is because the window of opportunity for their personal success is short and the learning curve is long. From age 1 to 25, we live in a discovery phase, determining our personal mission and our place in society. From 25 to 35, we grow and build our career and experience. This does not usually produce a great income. From 35 to 55, a mere 20 years, we have the best income earning phase. Earning great personal wealth is still statistically low, so the emphasis should be on group success. Age 55 to 65 is a period of some ease and less work due to an achieved mastery. Saving for one's later years is critical now if it hasn't been achieved yet. Age 65 to 75 is the largest give-back period where our accumulated wisdom, mastery and wealth are relinquished. This final stage has been observed in all successful societies and becomes the most valuable contribution of that society.

Time flies by, it really does. And we make many mistakes along the way. Why not teach the children before it is too late for them to spend their life energy wisely?

Earn-traprenuers

The foundation of this country was built on entrepreneurism. Settlers, religious pilgrims and other entrepreneurs left their enterprises in Europe to create new ones on unknown soil. Colonists came for many reasons: to flee excessive and arbitrary taxes, poverty, diminished opportunities, dissension, religious persecution, excessive regulations and impositions by tyrants and despots. Some were criminals in the eyes of the Crown. They took the opportunity, some at great risk to their personal lives and family, to create a new economic, legal and religious equality. That is the economic, legal and religious equality we need today, 21st Century Style.

Keep in mind that these pioneers and risk-takers did not have a lot of credit. They had to build from ingenuity, persistence and what cash they brought. Businesses were cash based. That is how commerce took place. This is important. They did not have their business income reduced by retail taxes or regulatory fees and they did not pay personal income taxes. From the shoemaker to the candlemaker, to the printer, the silversmith, the tailor and the farmer, these people simply exchanged goods for money or they bartered for essential services without being taxed. Colonial enterprises grew without the imposition of taxes from the first settlements in Jamestown (1607) and Plymouth (1620) until 1765 when the Stamp Tax was invoked, reducing the value of the money and their efforts to support themselves.

I mentioned my professor in Section Four. He made a huge impression on my life by making it abundantly clear that all we really have in life is the ability to earn an income. Our most important asset is not our real estate, our stock portfolio, our inheritance or savings account. Nothing in life is secure if we can't earn a living. It is our focused life energy that gives us income and value in society.

As a side note, we hear a lot of encouragement today to follow our passions. I don't want to degrade the value of passion, but passion doesn't usually drive economic realities. Please don't go down that rabbit hole. You can have a tremendous passion for any number of personal interests, but will you trade those for your ability to provide for the people that depend on you? Without a strong commitment to making a contribution to others that earns you an income, you become dependent on others. Dependence is an insult on our mutual needs. Passions are as likely to divide us as provide a satisfactory income.

In Cash We Trust

We have observed that cash based businesses are a poorly understood yet real opportunity for small businesses. I am sure that you also recognize that the government is not making it easy for small businesses to prosper. This can be traced to the layers of government regulations, taxes and reporting procedures. As a result, some owners employ the tactic of handling more cash just to make ends meet.

Here is the math: a cash dollar is a full dollar; a dollar earned through credit and debit cards is weighed down with various and multitude access fees and "discounts." Subtract from that dollar the costs of full reporting to comply with tax laws, licensing, possible franchise fees and federal, state and local business taxes.

Now the dollar earned has a value closer to 50 cents.

If, however, every dollar taken in is worth a full dollar, day after day, week after week and year after year, the comparative effect is like doubling the income every transaction. Owners of many cash based businesses have been doing this since the country's first colony and several have been able to stay in business year in and out because of this principle alone.

As a comparison, let me make a comment about compound interest and the "Rule of 72's." The Rule of 72's states invested money can double by a factor of the interest rate divided into 72. For example, a dollar can grow into two dollars in 12 years if it is saved at 6% interest. (Six goes into seventy-two twelve times.) Now, which makes more sense- compounding the untaxed dollar today or

188

compounding interest over a course of years?

> How many sides does a dollar bill have? Two, the front and the back, right? But in my book, a dollar bill has six sides. There are four edges: top, bottom and two ends. You may think those "extra four sides" are insignificant but they illustrate that money is multidimensional whether you realize it or not.

I have never operated on a primarily cash basis. I first read about it in Robert Kyosaki's <u>Rich Dad, Poor Dad.</u> Even if I haven't done it, I think it is important to discuss it with owners of small, family-owned businesses. I know that hair dressers, liquor stores, artists, donut shops, bowling alleys, landscapers, tattoo shops, accountants, dry cleaners, mechanics, cab drivers, food services and farmers have used cash to make their living. Now you know why they simply prefer cash.

Here is the caveat: operating a cash business may precipitate IRS attention. Common sense deems that if you are expecting that possibility, "give unto Caesar that which is Caesar's." But cash remains king for the entrepreneur. Perhaps the biggest value of a cash sale is that the cash remains such as it is, with all its inherent advantages, as long as, and until, taxes and fees are paid.

A cash-based business style is one criteria to look at when considering a niche market opportunity. Niche market opportunities often have one or more of these characteristics:

- cash-based,
- not highly regulated,
- under the radar businesses (no storefront and low overhead),
- too new to be visible to bureaucrats,
- serve a real, under-served and consistent business or personal need,
- offer considerable savings over the competition,
- a word of mouth business not dependent on advertising,
- minimal set up costs,
- clientele that prefer cash to credit.

When you think of these operations, you may think of fly-by-nights, illegal commerce or organized crime. I am not remotely suggesting that you operate like any of those. But the principles by which these underbelly entrepreneurs make huge amounts of tax-free cash are not all unethical.

If the trade for cash is value for value, and it is done with integrity, where is the problem? For example, an out-of-work carpenter needs to put bread on his table. He knows a neighbor, or a friend of a neighbor that needs his roof patched. Hiring a general contractor to bring in some subcontractor may cost the homeowner more than he is willing to pay. As a favor to this carpenter, the work gets done for half the price and done well. This keeps the carpenter off the unemployment rolls for another week (a savings to taxpayers) and he retains his dignity.

In an ailing economy where the regulations work against self-reliant entrepreneurs and officials have their hands out to save their jobs, what is really wrong here? Wouldn't *you* hire a good carpenter in order to help a friend or a neighbor of a friend? It's a roof patch, not an unsafe building addition trying to cheat the current safety code!

Could a car mechanic do something similar? A hair dresser? A street performer? Do you cry that they need to pay their fair share of taxes? If it is not fair then why is it okay that two thirds of Fortune 500 corporations (the richest corporations, I remind you) have not paid any taxes in

2009?[38] Or how did the other one third get their taxes reduced? What makes that okay for them but the hard working service provider has to pony up?

Cash-based businesses range from in-your-face corporate controlled casinos with massive amounts of cash changing hands to single-practioner nail salons and everything in between. Most of the ones I know take in a percentage of untaxed cash. Don't think for a moment that the casinos are reporting all of their income! The IRS doesn't have meters on every slot machine. In fact, IRS agents may be right there, standing by to take the names and social security numbers of jackpot winners. Even so, we have certainty that the casinos do not report all of *their* jackpots.

National pizza chains actively attract business people into this line of work. The new franchisees are often in it for one reason only...a large part of their business will be in cash. And don't forget the immigrants that come to America and make it big. Their successes are part of American lore. Yes, their success is a result of hard work, but even with a language deficit, they understand the language of cash. They choose businesses that can allow them to grow

---

[38] The Speech, by Senator Bernie Sanders

quickly on a cash basis.

The word about this opportunity brings many business start-ups to our shores. You will see various ethnicities operating liquor stores, gas stations, convenience stores, ethnic restaurants, laundries, food stands, nail and beauty salons, importers.... Some taco stands make $100,000 a year of untaxed income! Investing that into another salon or shop and it is compounding non-taxable income! It doesn't matter if you are making $150 or $500 per day. If it is there day after day and year after year, it acts like $300 a day or $1000 a day. Every dollar earned with cash is a full dollar you can spend or invest, not as a discounted taxed dollar.

You are probably aware that the wealthiest people do not pay taxes. The tax structure is created that way. The 1031 exchange is a perfect example of "tax avoidance" technically referred to as a tax deferment. The 1031 exchange in the IRS code allows property and land owners to exchange like for like properties and defer the payment of taxes. I have used it many times. It allowed me to legally avoid paying taxes. The wealthy claim 1031s with shopping centers, spec homes and development projects to legally avoid paying taxes. I am sorry if this offends you, but often, this is how millionaires are made. Read <u>Rich Dad, Poor</u>

<u>Dad</u>.

Niche Market Opportunities

Niche markets to an entrepreneur are like pollen for bees. They are satisfying, too, because they remain the best opportunities to make honest money on real community needs. One must get in a niche early and be able to sell it quickly because once the word gets out, competition quickly follows. The internet is both a help to find niches and a source of almost instant competition.

<u>The E-Myth</u> by Michael Gerber is an excellent source of information on making the most of niche markets. One of the beauties of niche markets is our large population base. You only need a small percentage of the population to earn more than breaking even. They don't require a large investment and do not require a complex delivery system. Gerber points out that by getting in early and designing the business to sell while it is still growing results in a preferred return on investment. Also, your profits won't be eaten up during the engineered economic downturns.

Niche markets follow trends and include grassroots responses to local and government failures and chronic regulatory overload. Opportunities exist because our skills training is falling behind the rest of the world. More opportunities arise because our systems ignore or miss needs such as affordable energy and preventative health care. Legal gobbledygook paralyzes the system and creates opportunities for consultants and action oriented groups. Under-served family issues such as day care and the need for flexible work schedules creates other trends. The rising costs of living are inspiring other trends and niches.

- Home schooling and tutoring
- Mediation and arbitration
- Online auctions and stores serving special interests
- Website development for niche markets
- Document shredding, document security and management
- Identity theft protection and consultation
- Credit repair
- Translation services
- Small business consultation
- Affordable health alternatives
- Computer security and data recovery
- Alternative housing

- Pick up and delivery
- Government contracting
- Care of senior citizens
- Document filing
- Health advocacy
- Mobile notary services
- Consulting businesses through the maze of governmental regulations
- Supplying the growing demand for medical marijuana
- Computer and cell phone applications
- Consumer advocacy
- Fraud alerts

Some of the above businesses can be mostly cash. Any business that doesn't make enough money to qualify for tax payments can also avoid paying taxes. Some businesses can pass along the recording and payment of taxes to other parties and avoid many tax entanglements. Here are some more cash based niche markets.

- Suppliers of art
- Renting of personal equipment to individuals
- Cash based finder's services

- Information research
- Street vendors
- Recycling
- Some consulting and management
- Speakers
- Donation based work
- Cash crops
- Computer based services
- Security and home assistance
- Tour guide
- Metal hunting
- Digital recording and data storage backup
- Flea market and garage sales
- Online affiliate businesses

More trends can be spotted online. Search blogs and news sources like Yahoo that report keyword search word trends. YouTube and Twitter can also give you a line on what is making news and potential trends. "Trend watching" can also yield interesting Google search results.

Mind you, trends and cash businesses do not necessarily make "sure winners" and many will not make a living wage if not done with efficiency, goals and some expertise. My point is that these businesses can potentially make more than you would think. And if you compare the costs of working for someone else, as recommended in <u>Your Money or Your Life</u>, the pay may be comparable with a lot less job related sickness and stress.

Like we are doing with this book and as practiced by the early founding citizens, any New Economy entrepreneurs will have to practice new values: simplicity, economy, flexibility, observing of cycles, community engagement and dedication to freedom.

Community Business

One business we observed at close range doesn't make business its main focus. The "Twelve Tribes" see themselves first as a religious community. Over the years, they have grown impressively in numbers and business reach. The Twelve Tribes have a vision that includes and welcomes many outcasts from institutional Christianity. The welcome they offer is followed with work and community opportunities on their farms and restaurants. Every building and farm is built from the skills contained within the group, which builds community and momentum. Visiting the Yellow

Deli, their restaurant in Vista, California, we observed more than a deli: carpentry, murals, fountains, artwork, stained glass, furniture, stonework, mood lighting, ironwork and books printed by their own printer. They must have computer experts on hand to make wifi available, to run their website and manage their books. Everyone serves at the Twelve Tribes. Their founder, Gene Spriggs, served us (no celebrities) like every other waiter. Other servers came to our table, took an interest in the development of this book and gave us attention until WE were done with the conversation. This is NEVER seen in corporate models of food service.

I believe their success comes from many elements including a community atmosphere focused on service and finding a perfect niche for them to operate within. The niche for the Yellow Deli is serving wholesome organic foods, literally twenty four hours a day! I challenge anyone to find another place in America that creates this kind of atmosphere with these high standards of food preparation. Yes, they look like hippies and disaffected yuppies, but that has not stopped the almost constant flow of business to the

Yellow Deli in downtown Vista.[39]

This brings me to an important point. Many niche market businesses are started by one or two people who think they already know what the market is missing, needing and looking for. This is usually nothing more than self-delusion. The Twelve Tribes' businesses are not about following their passion, pursuing a pleasure or a dream from childhood.

Your business advantage may come from a developed skill, information, connections or an uncanny inner guidance system. And if this advantage is to get monetary results, it must be built on facts, not defended by feelings.

The Twelve Tribes, whether by design and consciousness or not, make their business decisions based on group collected facts of what they have to offer the public. It doesn't run on a feeling or vision determined by an out-of-touch central leader. The local tribe leader (there are twelve) is wise enough to let the group take an active role in the success of each venture. The group collects information and applies individual skills, along with a willingness to fill in where skills need to be learned, so not a single person can bring the enterprise to its knees. This is an example how a

---

[39] Wade Skinner (Mevaser) reminded us that the core of good communities is the family and the basis of a strong family is a solid marriage. I agree.

true collective can work. Special skills are welcomed and creative ideas are explored at Twelve Tribes, but no operation hangs on a single skill, idea or vision.

Communities are the best supporters of any business. Communities create loyalties, better ideas, investment and help a business evolve to a higher response. The RCMC economy is failing communities because it asks communities to serve the national or world economy instead of the other way around. Economies must serve communities. Keep this in mind when developing your niche market business because if the community doesn't know about you or understand your business, they have no investment in seeing you prosper. All the work of prosperity will be on your shoulders alone.

Community is strength. If you look at any great enterprise, it involved a community. Kingdoms and empires were established because tyrants and common people needed the strength of numbers. The great religions of the world developed and served communities. The Revolutionary War in 1776 depended on communities because the freedom they sought would serve that community better than the empire. The Civil Rights movement was not about Rosa Parks or Dr. King. It was won by blacks and whites coming together in communities. The freedom India won from Great Britain was not the work of Mohandas Gandhi. Maybe it was his spark, but it was the action of communities that brought the victory. Monarchy ended in France as the result of communities in revolt, demanding justice for their communities. The Sisters of Charity have changed the urban landscape because they work in service to the unmet needs of hundreds in urban squalor. If your service is to be successful, its strength cannot be in your idea alone.

Integrity at the core

Integrity is of the utmost importance to any thriving community. No enterprise or community can stand long with its integrity in question. (See Section Four.)That is why we are at this historical opportunity. Americans are losing faith in the integrity of government, lawyers, police, schools, churches, the monetary system and so-called experts of economy. Where will they put their trust now? It is time to take responsibility, to take action and to work together on the new American economy. I hope it focuses on integrity. Any declaration or manifesto we make must appeal first to integrity.

Yes, we must demand integrity of our leaders and

institutions. Recall that the Founding Fathers insisted on the separation of Church and State. That was because the integrity of either is compromised by the influence and involvement of the other. They had seen it too closely to believe otherwise. Today, for the sake of the integrity of both, we must uphold the separation of Church and State. Hopefully, we are evolved enough now to know that morality and goodness cannot be legislated and God does not sanction any leader or particular type of government.

As a side note, it bothers me that some religious people think that they or their allegiance is "not of this world." Their apparent rationale is that Spirit is "good" and flesh and the world are "bad." Here's the rub: avoiding being involved in "the world" allows the RCMCs and the governing powers license to harm other earth citizens, or to steal resources and rule without consent. After all, it's bad and going to the devil. Right? If that is your position, then you can't take action or feel involved, so I am asking you to get out of the way of responsive earth citizens. If you want to sit on the sidelines, or allow the rape and pillage of our limited life-sustaining resources, get out of our way. Let those who profess to be "of this world" be the stewards of this beautiful creation.

Unlike those that believe the hereafter is their only hope, the Entrepreneur That Could belief is positive in the here and now. Our earthland home has all that we need to live a wondrous life and we have no doubts about what it takes to sustain life. There is no guesswork about what needs to be done, but we do know that there are plenty of people in the way of getting it done. What foolishness it is to not cherish, protect and nurture our very source of physical life!

Additionally, some institutional religions get too involved in our political and economic systems. Their beliefs have helped justify the rape and pillage of national wars. Why have they been silent when human rights are violated and abuse is evident? For instance, Lutheran and Roman Catholic congregations did very little to stop Hitler from killing Jews, the elderly, Jehovah's Witnesses, Gypsies and the handicapped. Recently, we have seen how bishops and other church authorities hold back the truth of child abuse, alcoholism, embezzlement, adultery and fraud. The Founding Fathers had the common sense to keep institutional religion out of the founding documents and structure. Religion is a personal matter that doesn't belong in business, government or other community services.

Similarly, the integrity of government is undermined when any branch of government is more powerful than another. We can tell by the actions of some of our Executive leaders that think they are above the law of Congress. Branches of government add departments to extend their power and to override their dependent cooperation with the appropriate branch. This is not integrity. We have no obligation to be governed by "representatives" that make their own laws for self-benefit.

Sullying the integrity of each branch of government is Wall Street. Their experts sit in chief administrative positions, pay our representatives to vote in their interests, take judges on junkets and fly them to pricey seminars. The results include:

- Prolonged, unwinnable wars to protect the capture of international resources;
- Wall Street holding our government hostage;
- Wall Street operating without the consent of the people;
- Wall Street writing legislation and
- Wall Street creating international trade policies.

In so doing, the government/ RCMC merger has failed our

children, our future, our health and our economy every bit as much as permitting a merger of church and state. This has developed into *Business Incapacitation, Overtaxation, Militarization, Legislation, Regulation and Dehumanization without Representation.* Who could find integrity in that?

We can oust Wall Street, those thugs of finance that have burdened us with unconscionable debt. We can do this by withdrawing funds from Wall Street, boycotting the major producers of fake foods, and investing in our local economies. We can declare our independence from the bargain makers that leave us with a bill too large for our own generation to pay. We can demand integrity and transparency of our elected officials' dealings with big business. We can choose only those products that respect our planetary resources and neighbors.

Risk or Opportunity

Is creating our own common future too risky? It is an important question. What is your health worth? It is at risk now with out-of-control pollution and unrelenting stress. What is our children's future worth? How much should we risk making their futures better? What risks do we face if the RCMCs and our politicians continue to offer lip service to our real needs? Wouldn't we rather welcome the opportunity to work closely with our neighbors than being married to name brands and sound bytes that tell us only what they want us to know?

Yes, declaring our independence from Wall Street will threaten many of our conveniences (especially our addiction to salty, sugary and fatty foods) as well as some of our jobs. There will be fewer cheap goods on the store shelves, fewer convenience stores and Wal-Mart may have to cut back. It will cost more to buy gasoline, but we may car-pool more efficiently and get to know our neighbors on the way.

I think it is important to realize that we need more than conveniences and goodies to make our lives meaningful. We need one another more than the trappings of class and attainment. We need to recall our great American advantage, being innovators, do-or-die initiators and hard workers that are committed to equal success without government intervention.

Besides American know-how and common sense problem solving, our risks can be reduced by our ability to look problems in the face. We further reduce risk by acting sooner than later and by working together instead of allowing ourselves to be divided. Risk rises with neighborhood name-calling and finger-pointing. Risk is reduced with clear headed thinking accomplished with organic, healthy food. Risk escalates when good people are denied equal access to life's sustenance while others take their time resolving the problem because they need their vacation time in Fiji. We can reduce risk by creating opportunities for innovation, change and unconventional business models.

Our independence from Wall Street could very well create a new, and healthier connection with Earth, especially through home grown food and nutritional consciousness. I stand by this promise: we will be more amazed by the joys of community and sharing food than we ever were amazed by television and prepackaged dinners. We will sleep better, have more community and personal pride, make love more often and have more energy. We will laugh more, forgive more and be more when we are fueled by nature's fresh air, soil and sunshine. My life is always more energetic and my commitment to life is stronger because of the refreshment and recreation offered by being with nature.

The Positive First Steps of the Revolution are throughout this book.

Our call for a Jeffersonian revolution is a call for common hope, responsibility and possibility. We need community effort and consciousness, Founding Fathers' style. But this revolution is not for our individual benefit; it is for America's next generations and for everywhere that people want common prosperity and shared resources.

I list the major steps below. If many of us will take these steps now, a revolution of the violent kind may be averted.

- Start growing at least some of your own food.
- Eat nutritious food only.
- Turn off the TV.
- Start healing the RCMC divide by uniting with neighbors, coworkers and community supports.
- Act with knowledge that our action now is not about us, but is for the children's future.
- Watch trends that your skills and experience will be able to use as a niche market opportunity.
- Encourage the sharing of local resources and inventive solutions. Buy at Farmer's Markets if your

town has one.

- Boycott soft drink companies and junk food.
- Keep your religious views and practices private. This is respectful of others. If your faith requires proselytizing, let others ask you first about your spiritual resource.
- Read daily from the Founding Fathers, especially Thomas Jefferson, Ben Franklin and Thomas Paine.
- Use more common sense.
- Drive the car less, share the car more, live by public transportation routes, walk or bike to work.
- Hire locals first. Buy local first.
- Start and finish these books to put your money and business in order: <u>Your Money or Your Life</u>. <u>The E-Myth</u>. <u>Rich Dad, Poor Dad</u>.
- For health and nutrition, read <u>The China Study</u>.
- Watch these documentaries to understand the present rule of RCMC's: Food, Inc., The Corporation, Zeitgeist.
- For the joys of a simple life, read <u>The Complete Tightwad Gazette.</u>
- Don't read first and act later. Act now. The time is short.

We may have to do these "collapse preparations" as well:

Stock up on food and water (develop water collection strategies) to feed our family during the collapse.

- If medications cannot be stockpiled, keep backup over-the-counter remedies.
- As joblessness grows, house more than your immediate family in your dwelling. Create a tribe from this.
- Arm yourself to protect your tribe, food and shelter. This could mean guns and ammunition, bad attitude, watch dogs and perimeter alarms.
- Stock up on little things that it would be hard to live without such as shoe laces, emergency lighting and energy, soap, toilet paper, aspirin and writing paper.
- Necessary tools include buckets, sponges, nails, hammer, saw, pliers, scissors, tweezers, wire cutters, knives, writing tools, cooking tools.
- Stock up on multiple-use solutions such as string and rope, duct tape, flashing, baling wire, electrical cord, towels and rags, wood, garden hose, electrical tape, glues, packing tape, newspaper, thread and

needles.   You may notice that many of these solutions are to repair and adhere. Yes, things will be falling apart and there may not be affordable or new ones at the stores!

Are you revolution ready?

Will you continue the insanity of doing the same thing and expecting a different result? Or will you take the next steps for a true revolution of entrepreneurial success? Let common sense be your guide. Don't depend on money; it may only help to guarantee that you will suffer longer without a principle worth living for. Sharing this book with neighbors, coworkers and family will improve the likelihood of communal success. Visit our website for updates. It is up to each one of us.

This book in not the end

Sustainable business models must be put in place and allowed to proliferate. In ETC, you've read the philosophy behind a new American Dream. My commitment is to keep this conversation going, reporting on what is working and meeting with communities.

I thank you and my vision thanks you. You are the hope

for my children and grandchildren. You are the hope for this beautiful earth we all call home. Together, we can thrive...with integrity.

Niche Markets, Supplement One

What is a niche market?

Niche markets vary from the "all cash" mom and pop venture to the well structured, corporate modeled businesses like franchises and very successful sole proprietorships. A good example of an upper end niche would be a franchise opportunity with multiple stores and a high gross volume right in the middle of market demand. There are niche market opportunities anywhere in that range of self-employment.

Niche markets are unique because they bound by time. They last only two to five years. After that, unless there are trademark, copyright or patent protections involved, they are gone. Why? Because niche markets are identified by being exclusive, without competition. I would include some franchises as niche market businesses because their product or service is unique. Sometimes these franchises get absorbed by other companies, similar to how Kinko's was absorbed by Fed Ex. Kinko's started as a successful niche market offering copy services for college campuses. It established itself before our present day computer technology became ubiquitous. Their printing business model succeeded because efficient, large scale printing and binding had not been done before on campuses.

On the smaller end of the scale are retail businesses like restaurants, coffee shops, nail salons, hair salons, various kiosks and hot dog stands. Kiosks and food carts can operate in their environment without the typical brick and mortar overhead. Internet businesses can also be niche markets, especially those that are incorporating the ever growing and changing technologies.

On the trail of technology, we will continue to see a dizzying array of niche opportunities. Video and music technology blend beautifully with the internet, but the life span of these niches is shockingly short due to the intensity of the competition. We should continue to see many new technologies and variations of social websites, podcasting and real time reports combined with hot new personalities.

Not too far off we will see a convergence of TV, cell phone, video and computer technologies into one unit. That will offer opportunities for applications developers. On the other hand, there is the possible intervention of commercial interests and the government, especially when the podcasts, video or other media expose more people to what is going on. Right now there is a legal battle going on over the right of people to video record and post on the internet the activities of police and other officials employed by the public.

Niche markets are sometimes confused with being a product or service to a targeted or niche audience. For instance, coffee shops and yogurt shops, while serving a more select audience than restaurants and fast food retailers, might not be niche markets when they do not have an exclusive product that is unavailable in the area. But a hot dog vender that caters to foot traffic and is the only hot dog vender in 3 square miles is a niche market. To be completely clear, a niche market is defined as a consumer or business need that has no competition. If it is a brand new, unproven idea discovered and developed by an entrepreneur, it is also a niche market. The completely new product is the kind of niche market that gets the most attention and can pay off the biggest, but it is not the only opportunity. The ideal niche market entrepreneur recognizes something nobody else is doing, then exploits it rapidly, getting as much growth as possible in a couple of years.

The beauty and brilliance to a niche market is having no competition. You have a lock on all of the demand. It's an entrepreneur's dream. You don't have to work as hard because all interested parties must come to you. Then, not too much later, you can sell this locked up market. Part of the attraction to a buyer is that the business has the economic foundation to support it long term. It won't just wash away like so many other small businesses.

By contrast, look at most small businesses in a shopping center. You will see that they aren't doing well. (The economic foundation is crumbling.) I have seen friends and family participate in the retail shopping center arena and I have seen what they do. They work their fingers and backs to the bone. And all they make is $40,000 a year. That is a waste of energy! And conversely, I have known individuals that own shopping centers. That was hot for several years, but it is going into reversion now because consumerism isn't supporting it.

Niche markets exist in **every** industry. Knowing something about that industry would clearly be an advantage. It would allow you to be aware of what is being offered and what is being missed.

Niche markets are now working in food and food production such as artisan foods and organic produce. I have noticed artisan cheeses being made for the market made up of the same five star chefs that demand culinary excellence. An older example of a niche food product is Ben and Jerry's Ice Cream. They focused on organic ingredients from family farms for improved flavor and unique flavor combinations. Their emphasis on social consciousness didn't hurt either. This niche is still working for them since 2000 AD when they were sold to Unilever.

My first niche

My first niche market was developing real estate in a way that no one else was doing. One other guy came in after me, but we were the only ones buying R-1 properties that were zoned for four units. What we did was leave the existing structure there and add three units to maximize the zoning density at four. The power, sewer and water infrastructures were left as they were. We were the first ones to do that. Technically, we were remodelers, but we came to this remodeling more as investors. The big builders didn't see that as profitable, so they left us alone. They wanted the large homes, the multi-unit developments and commercial projects like shopping centers.

So no one had done this before and exploited its potential. We got in there and built about twelve or eighteen of them without competition. Then the other developers saw that we were making $200,000 on these units in six months and they realized that this was a better return than their spec homes and with lower risk. The city tried to slow down our approvals, but the zoning allowed it. Sometimes there were local people that didn't want multi-family dwellings in their neighborhood because of fears of what it would do to their land values. And the historical society looked into what we were doing, but we made some architectural refinements that satisfied what they needed.

That was a niche market. Had I known more, I would have done it differently. It would have been smarter to buy up the various R-1 buildings and get the zoning approvals before developing. It would have been simple to get an investor to capitalize it with the entitlement approval. Having all of the approvals in place was when it actually became valuable. After that, anyone could have built three more units there. Doing this would have reduced our risk to almost zero. As it turned out several years later, both the nearby college and hospital expanded, making the multifamily housing a perfect solution for the community! We didn't see that coming.

This illustrates another aspect of niche markets. What makes the niche market so valuable is the opportunity to charge full price. There is no competition at first, so the buyers can't work you off of your competition. By the time the idea is being done elsewhere, the resource has been fully exploited.

The economic neighborhood

Another factor in niche markets is the way the economic neighborhood changes. Often these changes come around a blind corner. Depending on the change, the result can be disastrous or bountiful. If the change is negative, it is time to get out. But that's just the nature of niche markets.

I read an interesting example about a great niche market that exploded due to a change in the economic neighborhood. The business "1-800-Got Junk?" was just a couple of college guys looking for a way to make some money for school. There had been hauling services beforehand, but they didn't have an image. Brian Scudamore started with a beat up pick up. Not much of an image but he developed a look that distinguished him from other haulers. It included clean trucks, uniformed drivers, a toll free number, on time service and the offer to recycle the junk he could. In 2004, he had a 32 million dollar business with a goal of 250 franchise partners by 2006, according to www.about.com.

The economic neighborhood changed when the country's real estate market started tanking and hauling services were needed more than ever. They could never have predicted that. But because they had perfected their system and franchised it all over the country, they offered the best prices and service. Better still, they have grown and adapted almost completely from cash assets.

Growth in US cities is slow right now making strong economic neighborhoods hard to find. Even in the hottest US markets, such as Dallas and Houston, the growth rate is only 1% these days. The places in the US that are growing economically are in the oil rich regions, like Texas, Louisiana and Oklahoma. The corporate headquarters for the world oil industry are in those locations. They spend money on eating out, home improvement, cars, business conventions and parties, etc. Many new businesses are opening based on the demands of this hub of economic activity.

The other US market that is doing well right now, and I know it because it is right under my nose, is upper level college towns. Chapman College in old Orange has been expanding for the last two decades. It's a private college, and if you live in that area, you want your son or daughter to go there. It has a great economics department, music department... And it's expanding. So if you own anything in that area such as a restaurant, ice cream shop or bar...it's a bustling business. It wasn't like that twenty years ago when the college was small and didn't have the support for many restaurants.

I know one restaurant owner, Paul, the founder of Rutabegorz. The business started in old town Fullerton and catered to the Cal State Fullerton crowd with healthy organic food. He employs college students and they have a little hippie-type atmosphere going. Paul saw old Orange as being the same as old Fullerton with an expanding college and put one there by Chapman. Now he owns four of these restaurants and does very well. He created wealth from filling a niche. His niche is old town environments next to growing colleges.

Independent inside track

A tradesman I know focuses on wrought iron, which while being unique and specialized, is not necessarily a niche market. He flew over to England recently to see what his brother in law, who was making serious money, was doing. His brother-in-law, Kyle, is making some serious money there. Kyle sat on some city council and planning departments around London for six years. This allowed him to see what the city was letting out in the way of contracts. He saw contracts for everything from trash to janitorial, signage, development and much, much more. So he got to see all the people that were taking advantage of taxpayer supported services. While serving, he was thinking about the opportunities that were passing through. This alerted him to what opportunities would be out there when he returned to the private sector.

After leaving government service, Kyle was able to get a contract to provide janitorial and maintenance services to some of the city buildings. From there, he got another contract for additional work and then he sold his business to a large company that does this kind of work throughout London. He took the money from that sale, and using his former city contacts, started buying inner city lots that could be rezoned for mixed uses. Mixed use zoning allows residential, professional, office and retail uses in a single, multilevel building. It's just inner city redevelopment. So he would buy these tracts of land, get the zoning and entitlements and not even mess with the building. Then he sold the entire package to developers. The demand was there in London, but it could be done anywhere there is demand for mixed use buildings.

So being involved in the public sector was a great advantage to this businessman. By working for the government, he made contacts with those that had a budget for necessary services. We mustn't forget that London is a city in competition with other cities and the suburbs. It must deliver the necessary services, so it seeks out businesses to do that. The government sector has launched many a prosperous career.

Long term

Being involved in a community, such as serving on city council, is a good way to find entrepreneurial opportunities, but how else does one keep their ear to the ground to find trends and opportunities? What about listening to customers to find out what they are not getting from their present suppliers? Don't forget that it is just as important to recognize the components for long term success. You need foundational components in place, such as a well-funded but aging urban landscape or a growing college market to support the venture long term.

Each business must have supportive demographics that support long term success or the business is no more than a good idea whose time is not right. Look for established traffic and demographics before launching your business. For example, McDonald's has a consistent strategy they will not deviate from – even though they "own" the fast food market. Other franchises like "In and Out Burger" and "Burger King" follow the same model. They won't put their store in until the demographics are at a certain level. They might even contract with a developer to secure one of the pads with the highest visibility but delay construction for years. Only when the traffic patterns and their ideal demographics prove that the operation will succeed do they build. They may be monitoring traffic patterns, construction of ramps and thoroughfares or waiting out a recession.

Their criteria clearly spell out how many business and residential locations make their success a long term affair, what kind of businesses build there and the demographics of the residents. They know they can capture their market share once their criteria are established. They just won't take a chance on their market share not being there.

Internet Upstarts

Now that the internet is in full swing, the demographics for the economic foundation element has shifted. And we still don't know how this will fall out, but we do know the internet use will increase. We will see some government and corporate restrictions coming in, but it's not certain how that will play out.

It would be interesting to look at the numbers of internet based niche businesses that succeed. Particularly, how many internet companies have attempted to exist primarily via internet sales and how many have succeeded? Then, I'd like to hold those numbers against the SBA numbers. (95% of all small businesses fail in the first five years.) Are the internet based niche businesses "succeeding" at the same percentage?

And when the effects of peak oil change the marketplace,

what will that do to internet businesses? It won't necessarily be good for the internet. Peak oil will affect the global market and all participants in the marketplace. (That's you and me.) Of course people might be inclined to shop online more instead of driving their cars around to find the best deals but the costs of transportation for goods will inhibit every business. While the internet has changed the economic foundation by removing, or reducing, the necessity of a physical storefront, most profit still depends on the delivery of goods, which requires oil. The least affected by peak oil will be those enterprises that do all of their business online.

I am reminded of the shift created by automobiles at the turn of the last century. Before then, homes typically had three generations all participating in the economics as well as the household tasks of raising a family. But once the automobile became an affordable option, it was "suddenly" okay for the children to move out of the house, particularly move out west to seek a new opportunity. This redefined the family more than anything in thousands of years.

(You know, it benefits the large corporations for families to be apart. Two houses for the same three generations sells more cars, major appliances and consumer goods. That would be a house for the grandparents and another for the parents and their children. But even more homes and services result when the grandparents or parents divorce. More cars, more major appliances and consumer goods. Corporations have no financial interest in families staying together.)

Family Assets

I was thinking the other day about families and how they used to be seen as having an differentiating character. One family might excel at having great holiday decorations and celebrations. Another might be a wealthy family. Another could be known for their religious convictions or commitment to education. That was the family's identity and the children became a product of that environment.

One family, the Bakers, had weekend excursions that left an indelible impression on me as a child. Sometimes, on my journey to elementary school on a Monday morning, I'd see their open garage and I'd see them unloading their stuff from their weekend activity. One time it was fishing poles. Later, I saw rocks and Indian artifacts they'd found. Another time I heard about their gold panning travels. It was like an adventure every time I walked by their garage. Sometimes a crowd of kids would gather around and listen to the stories of their latest adventure. We'd see fish they'd caught or a skinned rattlesnake. And for kids, it opened our eyes to what was possible. But you don't see families having those kinds of identities much these days. Those family traditions are rare and less valued. Grandparents used to have a huge impact on the grandchildren, bringing traditions and solid wisdom that could help those kids make the most of life.

Today, we are not known for our family traditions, uniqueness or strengths. We are all happily adopting the one corporate tradition: Consumerism. We define ourselves by the clothes we wear, the kind of car we drive, the technology we own, the schools we go to, the house we live in (the outside of it more than the inside)... To me it is a valueless tradition. There is nothing of worth there. It is superficial.

I was fortunate enough to grow up in a community that started out as an agricultural community and turned into an affluent community filled with entrepreneurs of all kinds. From professional athletes to builders and developers, to manufacturers to doctors. It was really interesting to grow up in that community. It became a tradition of entrepreneurism.

One group of doctors in our community had a group practice that was successful enough to generate a lot of money to invest. They put an investment group together and I played Pop Warner football with one of their kids. He eventually became one of their main investment strategists. He had a real knack for making money. The doctors were busy with their practices and family and left my friend in charge of some investments. They ended up funding some purchases of black market grenades, rocket launchers and machine guns for African insurgents. It's not that they were ignorant of what was going on, they went ahead and justified it with their political belief system. They believed it was about spreading democracy, but those wars were really about corporate takeover, destabilizing governments in asset rich areas so their resources could be captured. I knew back then that that was ugly.

But there were many other entrepreneurs in my home town. One of them is running for Mayor of Anaheim. It's a big city in Orange County, and the revenue from Disneyland keeps pouring in. Years ago, his father had a degree in engineering and his company would change out the gas tanks at gas stations. You know, the tanks that were made out of metal had some corrosion going on, and the galvanization process, as well as the welding, caused some leaks. The petrochemicals would seep into the ground water, contaminate wells and the water supply system. He replaced the metal tanks for one gas station with composite or polyurethane tanks and then started doing it for other stations. They would close the station for a couple of weeks, bring in the heavy equipment, get rid of the hazardous waste and install the new tanks. He charged a lot of money for this service. This is a niche market with almost no competition. Those kind of entrepreneurial stories were all around my town.

Shopping developers and home builders were my neighbors, too. I went to school with one of the daughters of the Shea Home business. That's how I got into development. So the entrepreneurial spirit was alive and thriving in my town during the 70's and 80's. Many of us saw first hand and were inspired by the entrepreneurial spirit whether we started out as "haves" or "have-nots." Just by exposure to this environment, the "have-nots" (myself included), worked all the harder to live the success we saw around us. And we had the economic foundation to support our efforts.

My father told me that is why he moved out from East LA, to get us kids in an environment that would have a positive effect on us. So, instead of seeing junk yards, apartments and ghettos, we saw development and tremendous change. He did that knowing that environmental exposure can be a huge influence on a child. I agree that we are all are products of our environment. In our case, some of the "have-nots" succeeded more than the "haves" because they had more drive. So, it takes exposure, drive and foundational elements for growth in order to succeed. Keep in mind, if the economic base is not there, the drive to succeed may end up being just a life of hard work.

One of the families we grew up with started as chicken farmers. The grandfather grew chickens and had three markets for them: the eggs went to the grocery markets, the chicken dung when to the crop farmers and the hens that were older, and no longer laying, went to a national fast food franchise. (The way the chickens are cooked under pressure makes the toughest meat pretty tender.) This made a decent living for him until the larger chicken farms came in and changed the market value. That's when he left chicken farming for a fresh niche. He turned the chicken farm into one of the first-ever "cut your own Christmas tree" fields. Because the area was affluent, the residents were okay with buying a fresh cut Christmas tree for $35 to $125.00. Eventually, the property became valuable enough to sell off and the Christmas tree farm was moved further east. The old chicken farm property was sold for a nice price to a tilt-up developer. (Concrete tilt-up buildings for industrial use.)

Grandpa didn't give up his Christmas tree business yet because it was still a successful niche. He needed a couple of years to reestablish his crop but he found a place to grow them that was almost free. Because of a connection the family had, the trees were allowed to grow under the high tension electric utility lines. The lease for the land was low due to the fact that there were not many other uses for the land and the land owner liked that the trees helped manage the landscaping. That tree farm accounted for the second generation's living. They held on to it for a long time because the low cost of growing the trees kept their prices competitive.

When the third generation took over, that niche had gotten too crowded and competitive. They transitioned to pumpkin patch farming, creating a local amusement spot with a harvest theme for two months a year, which grossed

60 to 80 thousand in that window of opportunity. One of the other brothers started the palm tree growing farm, and this was very profitable as long as there was a lot of development going on. Another niche market. Who would have thought that Christmas trees, palm trees and pumpkin patches would have created a good lifestyle for three generations? It will be interesting to see what these entrepreneurs get into next.

What do you call a gathering of crickets? A niche?

Another cool story is about a million dollar cricket farm. I found out about it because I fish with crickets and my son needed them to feed his reptile pets. We would go to the local pet food distributor, I think it was Petco, and purchase our crickets. One time when we were there, we saw a kid bring in these bags of crickets and sell them to the store manager.

So I got curious and started inquiring about the story behind that. The crickets were maybe 25 cents to a dollar depending on the size of the bag. The manager back then told us the story that the kid had a few reptiles and his dad was short on cash and told his son that he would stop paying for the reptile food. "Get your own crickets," he told the boy, "or get rid of the reptiles. I don't care if they are a quarter a bag, I just can't afford any extra expenses."

The young guy, who didn't want to lose his pets, went to the library and got some books on raising crickets. He realized that they were pretty easy to manage. He grew them in an aquarium, tossing in only a piece of potato for food and they prospered. The next thing you know, he had too many crickets. The young man, who was only 15 years old, sold some to his friends just to keep the cricket population down. They were only a quarter a bag, but they were needed every week. When the crickets multiplied even more, the dad suggested he take them to the store because he was getting worried about all the crickets.

But the store already had a cricket supplier in Arkansas. And yet, the price seemed good, so she started buying a few to help the kid out and to save on shipping. She showed the boy how to package them so they looked like the other crickets she sold. As the kid's cricket count went down, his dad realized that he had an extra $50 a week coming in from the crickets. So he talked to the manager and she told him that if he could deliver as a business, not as a hobby, she would talk to her other franchise store managers and see if they were interested. She insisted on the agreed packaging and demanded that he never come in short of what they needed!

The father and son conferred, built cages, covered them with plastic and the crickets multiplied like crazy. They didn't know it, but there was only one large cricket supplier in the country, so there was a hole in the marketplace. Before you could say "Jiminy," the dad was driving all over San Diego, Orange County and Los Angeles with a station wagon full of cricket bags. By that time, he was making making $2500 to $3000 a month cash. Pretty soon, the cricket farm in Arkansas began wondering why their business had dropped. They called the corporate executive of this pet store chain and asked what had happened.

That's when the corporate office got involved and started asking the Southern California stores why procedures had altered. And the manager I had been buying from told corporate, "Well, the crickets are 25 cents cheaper so I am making the company 25 cents more each time I sell one. Is corporate okay with that?" So corporate said, "Tell us more. Where are the crickets coming from? Could they supply more California stores?" And yes, she thought they could. This got back to the cricket farm in Arkansas and they saw the writing on the wall. They had no choice but to buy the competition. They paid two million dollars for it! And the young man was barely sixteen at the time.

Niche evolution

Some niche market opportunities like the cricket farm happen without forethought, just being there at the right time and learning how to supply the demand. Other niche markets are completely organic, evolving and growing by adaptation. Another friend of mine started out by cutting rebar and making metal stakes for the construction industry. So he pre-cut rebar, punched holes in stakes and sold them to a couple of construction supply houses. He had very little competition and he made out pretty well. The company that was his competition was shipping their product from the Midwest, which raised the price significantly. Besides his reduced shipping costs, he wasn't greedy. He operated from a slim margin of profit.

Unfortunately, the construction industry fell off in the 90's and he wasn't able to get enough orders. That's when he noticed a way to adapt. One of the hot industries at the time was the cable industry. They needed to dig trenches for miles to bring cable TV into local households. They dug these trenches along the roadsides about three to six feet deep. But the problem they kept having was the dirt collapsing into the trench before the cable got laid. The trenches were narrow, running from 3 to 12 inches wide where the cable was to be put. And when the dirt fell in, very narrow shovels were required to re-dig the trench, but there was no real supply of them.

The cable companies started using a "sprinkler shovel" that is normally used for laying irrigation pipe and they basically bought out all the available shovels. Based on his experience, my friend started making the narrow shovels for the cable companies. Then he heard that the sprinkler shovels the irrigation industry was using were breaking because they couldn't take the weight of digging. So he adapted the narrow shovel heads for the irrigation industry. His company, North Star Steel, came from "nowhere" because he knew fabricating in metal and saw a need.

His main competitor bought him out for several million and he got out before the economic cycle dipped. I don't think even his shovels could have dug him out of this slump! His associates told him that he would never be able to compete with the shovels being made in China. He didn't listen and just started making these specialty shovel heads.

By seeing a hole in the marketplace no one but China was filling, and retooling to accommodate it, "Jack" built a building for the production, paid it off, then sold it and the business.

It's more than that

These are hopeful and true stories of what can be done with niche markets. But it's important to understand that the entrepreneurial spirit is not just about business, it's about being human and recognizing opportunities to adapt and improve within the day-to-day world. This is exciting and it challenges every aspect of who we are. Technological advances, societal shifts and ever-changing cultural demands are a part of where we live, the time we live in and what we do with our gifts.

Entrepreneurism represents the opportunity for humans to adapt and proliferate, raising humanity to a higher level. The spirit of any society should be entrepreneurial based, not corporate based as we are now. The corporate mindset has put a lid on our inventiveness, cooperation and even our basic humanity.

America had this gift of entrepreneurism they gave the entire world. We have added more international patents than any other society on the planet for decades. But that spirit is dying and needs to be reawakened. If we don't get back on the horse, the corporations will continue to set our agenda. The world will move toward collapse without us.

I am against the global marketplace. We are all on this planet together and we should be working together instead of competing for dominance. If we had a more level playing field where entrepreneurs and local small businesses had an equal chance in the marketplace, this country would be entirely different. I believe that there is enough commerce going on every day to put money in everyone's pocket. Competition is not the whole picture.

Why couldn't there be a legitimately managed fund for small businesses? It could capitalize small business ventures where you also have access to successful business owners as mentors. Why isn't there support from Wall Street to grow small businesses? We entrepreneurs are on our own out here!

I see a solution. Investors in Wall Street need to look at investing in Main Street businesses. I know that many don't trust Wall Street. Even the Blue Chip stocks are being hit. Now, for lack of a solid investment, they are putting their money in government bonds, but even that is pretty unstable. Look at both California, the largest economy in the US (and eighth largest economy in the world) and the country of Greece becoming insolvent.   Investors are looking for places to put their money. Why not create a safe place and way for them to invest in small businesses? The safest place to put money is in the real US economy. Small businesses account for 80% of the employment in this country. If it is true that 95% of small businesses fail in the first 5 years, let's fix that. It's not that hard if we change our paradigm.

The failure of small businesses isn't because we are stupid or don't work hard enough. (We work harder than any other first world country.) Our business model needs retooling. I recommend the improvements Michael Gerber wrote about in <u>The E-Myth</u>. (Systematize to maximize efficiency and marketing, avoid emotional entanglement and build to sell.)

And we must shift out of our consumer driven business paradigm. As we have discussed elsewhere in ETC, business that makes common sense reflects community priorities instead of global consumerism. With the capitalist/consumerist paradigm, the deck is stacked against small entrepreneurs. It should not be acceptable to us, in a democratic society, that small business, the will of its workers, is not flourishing. And that is what the Entrepreneur That Could is about. We have everything we need to succeed (and then some) once we change the paradigm.

Entrepreneurial Education

We have been told that to succeed you need to graduate from one of the elite business colleges like Harvard or Yale. But guess what, Bill Gates didn't finish college. Nor did Steve Jobs, Michael Dell, Larry Ellison, Sir Richard Branson and many others that are leading the economic revolution. A survey conducted by Bloomberg in 2010 shows that the school of hard knocks was the number one source (tied with the University of California) for CEOs of S&P 500 companies.[40] There ought to be successful intermediary programs that prepare people for business success. But the problem with a business degree these days is that it prepares you for a corporate job, not a Main Street, small town, standard of living career.

The myth of having a formal education, unless you are trying to get into a specific profession or business, has

---

[40] http://www.collegedropoutshalloffame.com/

some explaining to do. It is highly overrated. Traditional business education doesn't work for entrepreneurs. It's institutional and not focused on creative business ventures. Entrepreneurial education is a different thing.

Formal business education is ill-prepared to teach entrepreneurs how to adapt with the efficiency and speed needed to market in the new economy. The speed of change in business services, products and opportunities is unprecedented. As a globalized market, we are at the forefront of the biggest change humanity has ever seen. The emerging markets have changed everything we knew about business. It's not just new consumer markets, there are new markets for qualified workers, office, lab and manufacturing spaces. There is telecommuting, too, where people use public or personal space to complete their work tasks.

Economics of Globalization

Here is an example of how globalization is affecting the coming marketplace. One of the world's largest manufacturers of a biomedical product just built a huge complex in Southern California. The bids were crazy for the opportunities that came from this. The bids came from building subcontractors to local suppliers to food services. The building is 90% complete... and they are going to abandon most of it. They are moving the majority of their operations to South America where the office space is one tenth of the cost here. Their investigations discovered that the work ethic there is strong and technically skilled labor is readily available. Even with the construction loss, they will clear billions of dollars.

Technically skilled labor in India and Costa Rica is available for around $23.00 to $26.00 per day. Compare the equivalent skilled worker in America: it's $101 to $108 per day for this type of work. These people are hard workers, can read technical manuals in English and don't need retirement plans. The high literacy rate there means possibilities for expansion and replacement.

Like the controllers of the diamond industry find the best diamond cutters in the world in India, today's global corporations look high and low for these kinds of opportunities. The right formula for them is low cost workers with the right skills, preferably without having to do much additional training. Also important in the formula are close resources, inexpensive extraction and production as well as a simple means of delivery. They found that they can get governments/ countries to compete for the corporations' factories. The winning government gives the corporations access to premium land, tax incentives or breaks, reduced regulations and they provide the infrastructure. This can get the government good marks for job creation and they get reelected.

As long as the corporations have their way, this scheme is here to stay. A lot of our challenges are due to globalization under the corporate model. But beyond the corporate greed that we see demonstrated all over the world, globalization is the opportunity to bring employment to other cultures.

A recent article in the Costco magazine was about a man that makes shoes and boots employing third world labor. He is not taking advantage of the people because each person, village or tribe works at their own will and pace. The shoes are organic. The style has caught on so well that he now suffers from back orders and the market forces the price up for the less available styles. Consumers are buying multiple pairs at once to avoid any delay. That is a positive global marketplace.

There are some significant ground level opportunities worldwide. We can start with repairing America's economic vision. I don't see anyone else coming up with a vision of America's business future, so let the entrepreneurs do it and let's plan big! It could be to be..." "the bio-tech leaders," "the forerunners in new delivery systems," "the designers of carbon-free fuel," "the new age in aeronautics," "the leaders in transportation," "the high priests of technology"... Let's dedicate America's small businesses to keeping on track for a realistic future, not based on the failed model of free market consumerism. Let's bring the brightest minds in the world to our schools and communities for the ground level opportunities in the land of promise. Let's restore this country's purpose, as the one place in the world where you can start from scratch, make good and create a legacy for your family.

We know that the corporate model is, we can see it with Wal-mart. They are not going to save America because Wal-mart's intentions and priorities are global. Anyone with eyes can see that it is the corporations that destroyed our physical and economic landscape. The corporations don't care. They left us behind. They went global, left us behind and didn't even bother to look over their shoulder. They didn't look at the swath of destruction they left in their wake. Now they are hiding behind the curtains of Wall Street with their politician friends.

Get off our backs!

I love that more Americans scorn the sharks that are making obscene amounts of money. Their day is over. The people are more aware than ever that the success of these robber barons is on the backs of the less financially-abled and the less protected by the government. Shame on you, RCMC's. The celebration of greed is dying. The common values are shifting. Before too long, the Marie Antoinettes will be exposed and told to pay the price for their greed. It will be just like how the colonists tarred and feathered the representatives of the English crown. We are in such a mood now, that it will only take one event to trigger a movement that will turn this around for us. It may be violent, and maybe not. The trigger could be caused by a person or an event. In any case, people will just decide, "We have had it."

I advocate for a revolution that is positive in approach; it is the spirit of entrepreneurism that can save America. I believe that. America's future is in entrepreneurism, small businesses and community endeavors that serve their locality first. We can get America back through small business. We can demand massive community and legal support. We could use the kind of incentives and funding corporations leverage. And an ease on small business regulations is in order. Let's level the playing field, learn from fellow entrepreneurs, create a strong collective voice in government and stop the corporate economic manipulations that have forced us to fail.

The Entrepreneur That Could is working to create a network of alliances for America's entrepreneurs. We envision forums (online and in person), educational opportunities, economic campaigns and a host of communication venues. If you are serious about your financial and economic future, I encourage you to participate, reread and study the disciplines of ETC and draft your own declaration of independence from the RCMCs. I don't know how the future will play out with entrepreneurs at the helm, but I for sure don't trust my or my children's future to global corporations. And neither should you.

The US economic life preserver IS entrepreneurs on Main Street- small, community based, common sense entrepreneurs. That's the only hope.

Independence or Arrogance?

Supplement Two

Founding Father Patrick Henry challenged his colonial compatriots to stand against the growing threat to self-rule posed by the British crown. In the historical "Parson's Cause in Hanover County," Henry called King George "a tyrant who forfeits the allegiance of his subjects." A few years later, his career and family hung in the balance as charges of treason from his fellow Virginians forced him to declare his position, "I know not what course others may take; but as for me, give me liberty or give me death."

The Declaration of Independence (as copied below) lists more evidence of the overbearing British crown. (It is worth reading.) As a present day contrast, I invite you to look at the mounting evidence of class abuses compiled in <u>The Entrepreneur That Could</u> while sitting on that recently remodeled deck outside your multi-million dollar home with a view of the teaming masses below. Read "Plutonomy, Buying Luxury, Explaining Global Imbalances" like many wealthy investors did. (It is placed here in contrast to the Declaration of Independence.) It was written by world investment bankers at Citicorp.

What I see are bankers that have risen to the prominence of the royalty of old. They imagine that the world depends on them, their assets and their proclamations. To me, that is no different from the arrogance of King George.

Like Patrick Henry, I do not know what course my audience will take. But as for me, give me the right to prosper as an entrepreneur…or I will take it.

In CONGRESS, July 4, 1776
The unanimous Declaration of the thirteen united States of America

*W*hen in the Course of human events it becomes necessary for one people to dissolve the political bands which have connected them with another and to assume among the powers of the earth, the separate and equal station to which the Laws of Nature and of Nature's God entitle them, a decent respect to the opinions of mankind requires that they should declare the causes which impel them to the separation.

We hold these truths to be self-evident, that all men are created equal, that they are endowed by their Creator with certain unalienable Rights, that among these are Life, Liberty and the pursuit of Happiness. — That to secure these rights, Governments are instituted among Men, deriving their just powers from the consent of the governed, — That whenever any Form of Government becomes destructive of these ends, it is the Right of the People to alter or to abolish it, and to institute new Government, laying its foundation on such principles and organizing its powers in such form, as to them shall seem most likely to effect their Safety and Happiness. Prudence, indeed, will dictate that Governments long established should not be changed for light and transient causes; and accordingly all experience hath shewn that mankind are more disposed to suffer, while evils are sufferable than to right themselves by abolishing the forms to which they are accustomed. But when a long train of abuses and usurpations, pursuing invariably the same Object evinces a design to reduce them under absolute Despotism, it is their right, it is their duty, to throw off such Government, and to provide new Guards for their future security. — Such has been the patient sufferance of these Colonies; and such is now the necessity which constrains them to alter their former Systems of Government. The history of the present King of Great Britain is a history of repeated injuries and usurpations, all having in direct object the establishment of an absolute Tyranny over these States. To prove this, let Facts be submitted to a candid world.

He has refused his Assent to Laws, the most wholesome and necessary for the public good.

He has forbidden his Governors to pass Laws of immediate and pressing importance, unless suspended in their operation till his Assent should be obtained; and when so suspended, he has utterly neglected to attend to them.

He has refused to pass other Laws for the accommodation of large districts of people, unless those people would relinquish the right of Representation in the Legislature, a right inestimable to them and formidable to tyrants only.

He has called together legislative bodies at places unusual, uncomfortable, and distant from the depository of their Public Records, for the sole purpose of fatiguing them into compliance with his measures.

He has dissolved Representative Houses repeatedly, for opposing with manly firmness his invasions on the rights of the people.

He has refused for a long time, after such dissolutions, to cause others to be elected, whereby the Legislative Powers, incapable of Annihilation, have returned to the People at large for their exercise; the State remaining in the mean time exposed to all the dangers of invasion from without, and convulsions within.

He has endeavoured to prevent the population of these States; for that purpose obstructing the Laws for Naturalization of

Foreigners; refusing to pass others to encourage their migrations hither, and raising the conditions of new Appropriations of Lands.

He has obstructed the Administration of Justice by refusing his Assent to Laws for establishing Judiciary Powers.

He has made Judges dependent on his Will alone for the tenure of their offices, and the amount and payment of their salaries.

He has erected a multitude of New Offices, and sent hither swarms of Officers to harass our people and eat out their substance.

He has kept among us, in times of peace, Standing Armies without the Consent of our legislatures.

He has affected to render the Military independent of and superior to the Civil Power.

He has combined with others to subject us to a jurisdiction foreign to our constitution, and unacknowledged by our laws; giving his Assent to their Acts of pretended Legislation:

For quartering large bodies of armed troops among us:

For protecting them, by a mock Trial from punishment for any Murders which they should commit on the Inhabitants of these States:

For cutting off our Trade with all parts of the world:

For imposing Taxes on us without our Consent:

For depriving us in many cases, of the benefit of Trial by Jury:

For transporting us beyond Seas to be tried for pretended offences:

For abolishing the free System of English Laws in a neighbouring Province, establishing therein an Arbitrary government, and enlarging its Boundaries so as to render it at once an example and fit instrument for introducing the same absolute rule into

255

these Colonies

For taking away our Charters, abolishing our most valuable Laws and altering fundamentally the Forms of our Governments:

For suspending our own Legislatures, and declaring themselves invested with power to legislate for us in all cases whatsoever.

He has abdicated Government here, by declaring us out of his Protection and waging War against us.

He has plundered our seas, ravaged our coasts, burnt our towns, and destroyed the lives of our people.

He is at this time transporting large Armies of foreign Mercenaries to compleat the works of death, desolation, and tyranny, already begun with circumstances of Cruelty & Perfidy scarcely paralleled in the most barbarous ages, and totally unworthy the Head of a civilized nation.

He has constrained our fellow Citizens taken Captive on the high Seas to bear Arms against their Country, to become the executioners of their friends and Brethren, or to fall themselves by their Hands.

He has excited domestic insurrections amongst us, and has endeavoured to bring on the inhabitants of our frontiers, the merciless Indian Savages whose known rule of warfare, is an undistinguished destruction of all ages, sexes and conditions.

In every stage of these Oppressions We have Petitioned for Redress in the most humble terms: Our repeated Petitions have been answered only by repeated injury. A Prince, whose character is thus marked by every act which may define a Tyrant, is unfit to be the ruler of a free people.

Nor have We been wanting in attentions to our British brethren. We have warned them from time to time of attempts by their legislature to extend an unwarrantable jurisdiction over us. We have reminded them of the circumstances of our emigration and settlement here. We have appealed to their native justice and magnanimity, and we have conjured them by the ties of our common kindred to disavow these usurpations, which would inevitably interrupt our connections and correspondence. They too have been deaf to the voice of justice and of consanguinity. We must, therefore, acquiesce in the necessity, which denounces our Separation, and hold them, as we hold the rest of mankind, Enemies in War, in Peace Friends.

We, therefore, the Representatives of the united States of America, in General Congress, Assembled, appealing to the Supreme Judge of the world for the rectitude of our intentions, do, in the Name, and by Authority of the good People of these Colonies, solemnly publish and declare, That these united Colonies are, and of Right ought to be Free and Independent States, that they are Absolved from all Allegiance to the British Crown, and that all political connection between them and the State of Great Britain, is and ought to be totally dissolved; and that as Free and Independent States, they have full Power to levy War, conclude Peace, contract Alliances, establish Commerce, and to do all other Acts and Things which Independent States may of right do. — And for the support of this Declaration, with a firm reliance on the protection of Divine Providence, we mutually pledge to each other our Lives, our Fortunes, and our sacred Honor.

— John Hancock

New Hampshire:
Josiah Bartlett, William Whipple, Matthew Thornton

Massachusetts:
John Hancock, Samuel Adams, John Adams, Robert Treat Paine, Elbridge Gerry

Rhode Island:
Stephen Hopkins, William Ellery

Connecticut:
Roger Sherman, Samuel Huntington, William Williams, Oliver Wolcott

New York:
William Floyd, Philip Livingston, Francis Lewis, Lewis Morris

New Jersey:
Richard Stockton, John Witherspoon, Francis Hopkinson, John Hart, Abraham Clark

Pennsylvania:
Robert Morris, Benjamin Rush, Benjamin Franklin, John Morton, George Clymer, James Smith, George Taylor, James Wilson, George Ross

Delaware:
Caesar Rodney, George Read, Thomas McKean

Maryland:
Samuel Chase, William Paca, Thomas Stone, Charles Carroll of Carrollton

Virginia:
George Wythe, Richard Henry Lee, Thomas Jefferson, Benjamin Harrison, Thomas Nelson, Jr., Francis Lightfoot Lee, Carter Braxton

North Carolina:
William Hooper, Joseph Hewes, John Penn

South Carolina:
Edward Rutledge, Thomas Heyward, Jr., Thomas Lynch, Jr., Arthur Middleton

Georgia:
Button Gwinnett, Lyman Hall, George Walton

In contrast to the Declaration of Independence above, I thought the RCMC's "Declaration of Arrogance" (my term) should be reviewed as evidence. To read Citicorp's "Equity Strategy" newsletter of October 2005 is to get a wake up call. In the discourse called "Plutonomy: Buying Luxury, Explaining Global Imbalances" readers are allowed to observe the justifications of a mindset that few of us ever encounter. And if you had any doubt as to the veracity of my position, that the Resource Controlling Multinational Corporations have abandoned Main Street's small business entrepreneur, here is some damning evidence.

Citigroup, one of the international financial institutions that received billions of US taxpayer dollars in order to avoid collapse, previously promoted this theory on global imbalances. The theory proposed that global imbalances that upset their equity investors are "unwarranted." That is, when seen through "the prism of plutonomy," global investments are safer than common sense would justify. The "prism of plutonomy" posits that "global imbalances" do not sufficiently take into account the fact that it is the top few percents of economies that are the healthy consumers. The rest of the consumers are inconsequential. What appears as an imbalance is merely an illusion.

...the earth is not going to be shaken off its axis, and sucked into the cosmos by these "imbalances". The earth is being held up by the muscular arms of its entrepreneur-plutocrats, like it, or not."

What is a Plutonomy? Countries such as "the US, UK and Canada" "*where economic growth is powered by and largely consumed by the wealthy few."*

99% of the world is just "*the rest."*

The authors also predict more disparity between the rich and the poor in the countries that are so-called plutonomies. "*We project that the plutonomies (the U.S., UK, and Canada) will likely see even more income inequality, disproportionately feeding off a further rise in the profit share in their economies, capitalist-friendly governments, more technology-driven productivity, and globalization."*

This report has received a lot of criticism from egalitarian-minded people. Partly because of the obvious arrogance and partly due to the insult it is to the concepts of middle class and equal opportunity. Looking back over history to sixteenth century Spain, seventeenth century Holland, the Gilded Age and the Roaring Twenties, the mega-bank declares that plutonomies are possible given these elements:

"Disruptive technology-driven productivity gains, creative financial innovation, capitalist- friendly cooperative governments, an international dimension of immigrants and overseas conquests invigorating wealth creation, the rule of law, and patenting inventions. Often these wealth waves involve great complexity, exploited best by the rich and educated of the time."

This is the formula under which the RCMCs can proliferate and dominate. Read those again:

- technology that improves productivity as it disrupts former technologies and systems of economic and community support,

- financial innovations that improve the position of the wealthy and reduce the capital of "the rest,"

- governments that cooperate with and do not oppose capitalism even in its greediest forms,

- immigrant labor fleeing oppression and risking all in a new economic environment,

- overseas conquests (usually undertaken by governments or corporations sponsored by governments),

- the rule of law (laws that benefit dominating corporate strategies) and

- eliminating competition through patents.

Today, we also know that financial strangleholds are part of *"wealth waves exploited best by the rich and educated."*

The full report is 53 pages and can be found online. (Search "plutonomy") Please read the document. (I have not included all of it as I do not have the copyright.) In it, you will find statements like these:

"Fixing the global inequalities requires time travel to change fertility rates... or it would require making income distribution in the Anglo-Saxon plutonomies less skewed to the rich [which] would require revolutionary tectonic shifts in politics and society."

"There is no such animal as "the U.S. consumer" or "the UK consumer", or indeed the "Russian consumer". There are rich consumers, few in number, but disproportionate in the gigantic slice of income and consumption they take. There

are the rest, the "non-rich", the multitudinous many, but only accounting for surprisingly small bites of the national pie."

"Clearly, the analysis of the top 1% of U.S. households is paramount. The usual analysis of the "average" U.S. consumer is flawed from the start. To continue with the U.S., the top 1% of households also account for 33% of net worth, greater than the bottom 90% of households put together. It gets better (or worse, depending on your political stripe) – the top 1% of households account for 40% of financial net worth, more than the bottom 95% of households put together."

Does this sound to you like people that have equality in mind or believe that "all men are created equal?" Is it okay with you that these self-appointed drivers of the economy are telling themselves that what happens to them is really all that matters? Does this inspire you to go to their stores, agents or representatives and do business with them? Does it make you think that we are all on the same page? Do you think that this kind of imbalance is simply about the economy? Or is it also about who is best represented in government? Remember, according to Citicorp, small business entrepreneurs are just "the rest." And, for heaven's sake, is that the future for our children? Is this all we can offer them?

I recall what the colonists of the 1770's did to the British government officials. They tarred and feathered them. If they lived, they were shipped back to Britain in disgrace. Entrepreneur colonists put their lives on the line by signing the Declaration of Independence and continued their opposition until they were free.

When Citicorp reveals the *"entrepreneur-plutocrat"* mindset that small business entrepreneurs, their families, the people they employ and the communities they support do not matter to the economy, perhaps it is time for us to show them and their associates differently. Now is the time to begin the "revolutionary tectonic shifts in politics and society" that they named as necessary to fix the imbalance. Are you with me? Let us declare our independence from the plutocrats. Join the Entrepreneur That Could revolution.

www.TheEntrepreneurThatCould.com

Facebook: http://tiny.cc/facebook-entrepreneur
Email: info@TheEntrepreneurThatCould.com

Resources

> *...children believe everything their parents tell them. And as a result, they never learn to question things. Nobody questions things in this country anymore. Everybody is too fat and happy... We are way too *&#%* prosperous for our own good. Americans have been bought off and silenced by toys and gizmos. And no one learns to question things. -George Carlin: It's Bad for Ya, copyright 2008 MPI Home Video*

Books:

Rich Dad, Poor Dad, Robery Kyosaki

Your Money or Your Life, Vicki Robbin and Joe Dominguez

The China Study, T. Colin Campbell

The Emyth, Michael E. Gerber

Unequal Protection, Thom Hartmann

Author Marilyn vos Savant for development of sound reason and logic.

Four Arguments for the Elimination of Television, Jerry Mander

Civil Disobedience and Walden, Henry David Thoreau

<u>Into the Buzzsaw, Leading Journalists Expose the Myth of a Free Press</u>, Kristina Borjesson, ed.

<u>Propaganda</u>, Edward Bernays, endorsed by Noam Chomsky

<u>Breaking the News, How the Media Undermine American Democracy</u>, James Fallows

<u>War is a Racket</u>, General Smedley D Butler

<u>It Can't Happen Here</u>, Sinclair Lewis

<u>The Tightwad Gazette</u>, Amy Dacyczyn

<u>The Omnivore's Dilemma</u>, Michael Pollan

<u>Fast Food Nation</u>, Eric Schlosser

<u>When Corporations Rule the World, Agenda for a New Economy</u>, David Korten

<u>1984</u>, George Orwell

<u>Brave New World</u>, Aldous Huxley

<u>God Is Not Green</u>, P.D. Lingenfelter Highby

<u>The Death of Common Sense</u>, Phillip K. Howard

<u>A People's History of the United States</u>, Howard Zinn

<u>Ishmael</u>, Daniel Quinn

Internet:

TED.com for innovations and trends

Adbusters.org for serious criticism and comical lampoons

of advertising mania and rampant consumerism

ProjectCensored.org for coverage of censored news and insight into the RCMCs' dealings and related coverups

Corpwatch.com for international news of corporate operations and the consequences for others

Multinationalmonitor.com for monitoring RCMCs

Alternet.org for challenging the mainstream thinking on politics, media, environment, economy and more

StoryofStuff.com, for an overview of modern consumerism

The Story of Bottled Water found on the Story of Stuff website

Artwork of Chris Jordan, focusing on the rampant scale of consumerism, manufacturing and resource capture. Seen on Youtube, TED and his own site www.chrisjordan.com

YouTube: Search for "King Corn documentary," "Food inc" "The Corporation documentary"

Documentaries:

Food, Inc.

Food Matters

King Corn

The Corporation

Manufactured Landscapes

Zeitgeist

The World According to Monsanto

Capitalism, A Love Story

The Future of Food

Movies

Network

Being There

Fog of War

The Entrepreneur That Could   *Casey Jurado*

NOTES

www.ingramcontent.com/pod-product-compliance
Lightning Source LLC
Chambersburg PA
CBHW071403170526
45165CB00001B/167